The Ultimate

VITAMIX COOKBOOK
FOR BEGINNERS

Top 500 Superfood, Wholesome Vitamix Blender Smoothie Recipes to Manage Weight, Gain energy, Anti-age, Detox, Fight Disease, and Live Long

Patsy W. Moseley

Table of Content

Introduction..................1

Chapter 1: The Vitamix Blender for
Smoothies 2

The Basics of Vitamix Blender 2
Juicing vs Blending: What's the Difference? 4
Smoothies............................. 7
How to Get Started 12
Awesome Tips for Preparing Smoothies .. 12
Common Smoothie Problems and Solutions 14
Tips to Save Time and Money.................. 15

Chapter 2: Breakfast Smoothies 17

Nectarine and Orange Yoghurt................ 17
Papaya and Pineapple with Yoghurt.......... 17
Avocado with Kale and Coconut Milk........ 17
Kale with Milk Yoghurt.......................... 17
Vanilla Milk with Blueberries 17
Lemony Avocado Yoghurt...................... 18
Avocado with Pineapple Smoothie........... 18
Almond and Peach Oat 18
Coconut Milk and Egg Smoothie.............. 18
Almond-Chia Smoothie Bowl 18
Cocoa Mocha Milk Shake 19
Milky Strawberry Hemp 19
Overnight Almond Oats Smoothie 19
Apple and Milky Raisin Oat.................... 19
Coconut Flakes with Pineapple................ 19
Milky Chia Oat.................................... 20
Chia Cherry Yoghurt............................. 20
Cheesy Almond Milk with Avocado 20
Oats with Cashew Butter 20
Cantaloupe Berry Oat........................... 20
Banana Flaxseed Oat with Yoghurt.......... 21
Yoghurt with Pomegranate-Raspberry....... 21
Almond Milk and Honey Smoothie 21
Walnut and Banana Oat......................... 21
Limey Pineapple Yoghurt 21
Spinach and Flaxseed Smoothie 22

Almond Berry Smoothie 22
Cinnamon and Honey Smoothie 22
Milky Nut and Blueberry 22
Banana-Almond-Chia 22

Chapter 3: Superfood Recipes ...24

Milky Flaxseed Superfood Smoothie 24
Milk and Banana Oat Smoothie............... 24
Walnut with Almond Superfood Smoothie.. 24
Citrus with Chia Seeds Smoothie 24
Milky Superfood Berry Pudding............... 25
Buttered Maca Smoothie 25
Banana and Apple Berry Smoothie.......... 25
Spirulina Mint Superfood Smoothie 25
Berry Mint Superfood Smoothie.............. 25
Milky Cinnamon and Coconut Smoothie ... 26
Pineapple Hemp Green Smoothie............. 26
Vegan Chocolate Superfood Smoothie 26
Superfood Chocolate Cauliflower 26
Banana and Cacao Superfood Smoothie.... 27
Banana and Chocolate Malt Superfood
Smoothie 27
Blueberry with Mango Superfood Smoothie 27
Superfood Vanilla and Pie Smoothie 27
Superfood Spinach and Cucumber Smoothie 28
Spinach and Avocado Superfood Smoothie 28
Vanilla Berry Almond Smoothie............... 28

Chapter 4: Healthy Diet Vitamix
Recipes............................30

Vanilla Apple Caramel 30
Berry with Sweet Pea Smoothie 30
Nuts and Gritty Coffee Shake 30
Milky Cafe Banana 30
Lemony Carrot and Veggie Spice 30
Milk and Lemon Strawberry 31
Blueberry Ultimate Diet Smoothie........... 31
Cinnamon Raisin Bliss 31
Banana with Kale and Coconut Delight...... 31
Cheesy Almond and Banana Cream 32

Chia with Berry Carrot 32
Honey and Tofu Berry 32
Divine Chocolate Milk 32
Black Pepper and Pineapple Smoothie 32
Kale and Mango with Coconut Smoothie .. 33
Ginger and Tangerine Smoothie 33
Chocolatey Minty Spinach 33
Buttered Vanilla Yoghurt....................... 33
Cinnamon Banana Pumpkin 33
Tofu and Almond Chocolatey Date 34
Milk and Honey with Coconut Almond 34
Milky Flaxseed Spinach 34
Honey and Cream Berry Shake............... 34
Banana and Green Tea 35
Milky Strawberry Smoothie Sundae 35
Chocolatey Spunky Monkey 35
Chia and Banana Strawberry Peach 35
Watermelon and Berry Yoghurt 36
Strawberry and Ceylon Cinnamon Smoothie 36
Lemony Yoghurt and Sherbet Smoothie.... 36
Kiwi with Mango Smoothie 36
Spirulina Mango and Coconut Smoothie .. 36
Lime with Mango Greens Smoothie 37
Creamy Blueberry Bliss 37
Spinach and Grapefruit Smoothie 37
Stevia and Lemon Garden Smoothie 37
Grape and Green Tea Smoothie 37
Ginger and Strawberry Deluxe 38
Buttered Berry and Banana Smoothie 38
Almond Pumpkin Pie 38
Stevia Strawberry Hemp and Spinach Delight 38
Fruity Flax Seeds Smoothie 38
Berry Spinach and Apple Pie Smoothie ... 39
Banana and Limey Strawberry Smoothie .. 39
Creamy Berry Smoothie 39

Spinach Berries and Oats Smoothie......... 42
Carrot and Banana Crisp Apple Smoothie.. 42
Lemon and Milk Avocado - Swiss Chard ... 42
Watermelon with Minty Greens Smoothie.. 43
Flaxseed Green and Berry Smoothie........ 43
Vanilla Mixed Berry Yummy 43
Strawberry Sherbet Key Lime 43
Berry Spinach Green Smoothie............... 44
Minty Orange and Mango Green Smoothie 44
Kale with Fruity Green Smoothie............. 44
Milky Fruit Rainbow Smoothie 44
Kale Cherry Green Smoothie 45
Milky Soy and Green Smoothie 45
Peach and Honey with Kale Smoothie 45
Carrot Hemp Green Smoothie Bowl......... 45
Fruity Kale and Lemon Smoothie 46
Avocado and Apple Green Goodness 46
Cashew with Vanilla Apple Pie 46
Orange and Berry Fiesta 46
Tofu and Banana - Choco Split 47
Milky Banana and Butter Delight 47
Honey Soy Blue Smoothie 47
Vanilla Cashew Banana 47
Orange Yoghurt Citrus Joy 48
Fruity Grab Bag 48
Pineapple and Milk Flaxseed Supreme 48
Ginger Apple and Cucumber with Lemon... 48
Carrot and Apple Hot Tomato 49
Limey Mango Bliss 49
Berry and Melon Perfection 49
Chia Espresso with Vanilla Yoghurt 49
Milky Peach with Chia 50
Yoghurt and Chips Raspberry Treat 50
Carrot and Strawberry Oatmeal 50
Peachy Fruit and Yoghurt 50

Chapter 5: Weight Loss Recipes 41

Vegetable Fat Burning Smoothie 41
Apple with Chia Seed Smoothie 41
Vanilla Cream Avocado Smoothie............. 41
Berry with Green Vanilla Smoothie.......... 41
Orange and Red Banana with Yoghurt....... 41
Spinach and Creamy Banana Green Smoothie 42
Avocado Green Superfood Smoothie 42

Chapter 6: Anti-Aging Recipes...52

Vanilla Berry Anti-Aging Smoothie........... 52
Anti-Aging Turmeric Smoothie 52
Vanilla and Chocolate Berry Almond Blast . 52
Watermelon and Coconut Chia Smoothie... 52
Carrot and Turmeric Antioxidant Smoothie 53
Grapy Raspberry Antioxidant Smoothie..... 53
Parsley and Apple Anti-Aging Smoothie 53

Honey and Grape Goji Blast 53

Yoghurt with Watermelon Smoothie 53

Avocado and Berry Nice 54

Chia Berry Anti-Aging Superfood 54

Mango and Avocado Glowing Skin Glass.... 54

Strawberry Green Tea with Coconut 54

Milky Kale and Banana Delight 54

Lemony Carrot with Kale 55

Berry and Minty Coconut with Lemon 55

Milky Peach and Almond with Blueberry ... 55

Kale with Pineapple and Chia Express 55

Lemon and Mint Breezy Blueberry 55

Chia with Pineapple and Mango 56

Pear with Ginger Pure Gold 56

Banana and Almond Relaxing Oatmeal 56

Lemon and Milk Sunflower with Spinach . 56

Coconut Delight with Anti-Aging Turmeric 56

Goji Berry Wake Up Yoghurt.................. 57

Berry and Avocado Anti-Wrinkle Smoothie 57

Limey Fruit with Spinach and Cilantro....... 57

Nut and Berry Wrinkle Fighter 57

Lemony Kale and Carrot Glass 58

Mango and Pineapple with Chia Glass 58

Almond with Anti-Aging Cacao 58

Flaxseed and Orange Anti-Ultra Violet 58

Milky Sunflower and Fruit Green 58

Chapter 7: Detoxification
Recipes 60

Lime and Milky Detox Smoothie.............. 60

Lemony Green Tea Detox Smoothie.......... 60

Blueberry Fruit Detox Smoothie.............. 60

Turmeric and Cranberry Bliss Detox Smoothie 60

Ginger Avocado with Cucumber and Lemon 61

Pineapple with Kale Detox Smoothie 61

Ginger with Lemony Detox Drink 61

Minty Lettuce and Berry with Apple 61

Clementine with Carrot Detox Smoothie ... 61

Moringa with Hazelnut Detox Smoothie 62

Tomato with Zucchini Detox Smoothie 62

Turmeric with Carrot Detox Smoothie 62

Lemon and Pear Detox Smoothie 62

Lemony Chia and Ginger Beet 62

Swiss Chard Pineapple Detox Smoothie ... 63

Spinach and Avocado Detox Smoothie 63

Lemony Chamomile and Ginger Detox
Smoothie 63

Kiwi with Wheatgrass Detox Smoothie 63

Milky Almond Detox Berry 63

Ginger Lemonade Detox Smoothie 64

Apple Cider Detox Remedy Drink 64

Pineapple Matcha with Mango Smoothie.... 64

Cinnamon with Kale Power Detox Smoothie 64

Berry Spirulina with Avocado 65

Celery Mango Super Cleanse 65

Orange and Parsley with Mango Detox 65

Goji Berry with Banana and Strawberry 65

Banana Berry with Blue Ginger 65

Carrot Spring Cleaning Detox................. 66

Cilantro Algae with Kale 66

Ginger with Lemon Cilantro Detox 66

Peach and Mint Tea Smoothie................. 66

Cucumber Celery Cranberry 67

Maple Berry with Avocado Sunrise Smoothie 67

Lemon and Honey Tangy Blueberry 67

Lettuce and Mango with Lemon 67

Fruity Detox Special 68

Creamy Berry and Coconut Shake........... 68

Limey Cucumber with Cilantro and Kale ... 68

Berry Flaxseed with Dates 68

Milky Pear and Chia with Protein 69

Romaine and Avocado with Jicama 69

Minty Apple and Cucumber with Lime....... 69

Tomato and Spinach with Spicy Carrot 69

Chapter 8: Energy Boosting and
Protein Refuel Recipes 71

Banana Medjool Energy Smoothie............ 71

Fruity Energy Boost Smoothie 71

Blueberry Almond Butter Smoothies......... 71

Lemony Veggie Smoothie 71

Strawberry Watermelon and Honey Smoothie 72

Creamy Xanthan and Strawberry Smoothie 72

Yoghurt with Citrus Smoothie 72

Limey Yoghurt and Cinnamon Smoothie .. 72
Milky Chia with Mango Lassi................... 72
Cinnamon Yoghurt Energy Boost Smoothie 73
Almond and Mango with Honey Smoothie 73
Ginger and Pineapple Antioxidant Refresher 73
Cherry Protein and Coconut Smoothie 73
Kiwi and Fruity Green Tea Smoothie........ 73
Milky Flaxseed Berry Burst 74
Cauliflower with Raspberry and Chia 74
Milky Peanut Butter and Oatmeal Smoothie 74
Cucumber with Spinach and Orange
Smoothie 74
Lemony Cucumber Green Machine 74
Milk with Ginger Berry Flax Smoothie 75
Apple and Kiwi Green Goblin 75
Minty Yoghurt with Chocolate Chip 75
Kefir and Beet with Blueberry-Almond 75
Almond-Banana-Oat Recovery................. 75
Walnut and Peach with Cottage Cheese 76
Almond with Kale and Banana Power Protein 76
Pomegranate and Berry Energizing
Electrolytes... 76
Banana and Pumpkin Power Smoothie 76
Berry Yoghurt with Energy Superfood....... 76
Spinach Berry with Coconut-Fig.............. 77
Kefir Collagen with Cranberry-Orange 77
Kale and Fruity Yoghurt Refresher........... 77
Limey Banana with Coconut and Cashew .. 77
Avocado and Yoghurt with Blueberry-Pom . 77
Collagen with Peanut Butter Cup............. 78
Milk and Cinnamon with Cocoa Smoothie.. 78
Minty Cacao Stick Smoothie 78
Pineapple Berry Yoghurt Shake............... 78
Squash Persimmon Protein Smoothie 79
Chia Chard with Berries and Cream......... 79
Zucchini and Papaya with Toasted Coconut 79
Fruity Yoghurt and Avocado Blend........... 79
Watermelon with Beet and Yoghurt 80
Cucumber Hemp with Vanilla Revive........ 80
Milky Dandelion with Blueberry-Oat......... 80
Grapy Spinach with Berry Yoghurt........... 80
Kale with Yoghurt Ginger-Plum 81
Mango with Beets and Protein 81
Milky Beet and Cherry Smoothie............. 81

Chapter 9: Drinkable Snacks and
Desserts 83

Berry and Yoghurt Beets 83
Limey Grape Juice 83
Minty Grapefruit Juice 83
Radish Blueberry Blast 83
Limeade Cucumber with Cherry.............. 83
Pineapple and Peach Zinc Defense 84
Turmeric and Cauliflower with Mango 84
Coconut with Strawberry-Hibiscus........... 84
Chard and Cashew Berry Sage 84
Pumpkin Chai...................................... 84
Spicy Spinach with Pear and Kiwi............ 85
Minty Cucumber with Chia and Watermelon 85
Jicama with almond Milk....................... 85
Tropical Matcha 85
Kale and Celery Green Juice 85
Ginger and Almond Beets with Carrot....... 86
Yoghurt and Banana-Zucchini Bread........ 86
Layered Berries and Cream.................... 86
Guava and Orange Jicama Punch 86
Milky Chia Berry-Basil 86
Grapy Zucchini with Citrus Crush 87
Carrot and Orange with Coconut Milk 87
Cheesy Strawberry Hemp 87
Turmeric with Yoghurt and Lemon Tart...... 87
Garlic and Tabasco Juice........................ 87
Peachy Cinnamon Cobbler 88
Avocado and Banana with Chocolate Chip . 88
Berry with Pomegranate Sorbet............... 88
Almond and Banana with Pistachio Cream. 88
Cashew with Caramel-Covered Apple 88
Raspberries and White Chocolate............ 89
Lemony Celery and Parsley Green Juice ... 89
Beets and Carrot with Orange Juice.......... 89
Coconut Butter and Cherry Pudding 89
Cinnamon and Almond Milk with Eggnog... 89
Grape and Cucumber Green Juice 90
Squash and Dates Butter Pecan.............. 90
Organic Raspberry and Cucumber Juice 90
Apple and Ginger Carrot Juice 90
Lemon and Ginger Green Power Juice....... 90

Appendix 1: Measurement Conversion
Chart...91
Appendix 2: Recipe Index.....................92

Introduction

Vitamix is a high-powered blender that can do it all -- there is literally no limit to what you can do with this machine. The Vitamix is considered the Superman of blenders, you never have to ask the Vitamix "Will it blend?", because, thanks to the 2 HP (that's horse power) under the hood, you always know the answer. Yes, it will blend. Creamy soups, thick dips, sticky dough, dense cake batter, fruit smoothies, boozy blended drinks, DIY nut flours, raw juices made from whole fruits and vegetables, chunky nut butters—all of it will blend. And the list doesn't end there. The list doesn't end at all.

The Vitamix blends just about anything, grind nuts and seeds by completely breaking apart cell walls, turning them to dust, smash frozen fruit into a soft cream, warm up soups, sauces and dips by spinning them at a whopping 240 mph. It's a multi-function blender that can double as a food prep tool for grinding, chopping, juicing, and pureeing. With programmed settings on the Smart System Blenders, you can make recipes, such as smoothies and soups, while you tend to other things in the kitchen. With Vitamix, you'll also enjoy the versatility of size and strength. Using a Vitamix gives you the ability to make smoothies, frozen drinks and hot soups (depending on what you like).

Smoothies are a great way to enjoy food and at the same time get the nutrition that your body deserves. In this book, you will easily find recipes for all kinds of delectable smoothies and shakes that will not only get your taste buds satisfied but also your body as well. And with your efficient and reliable Vitamix Blender, making these smoothies will be a breeze.

The smoothie recipes in this book deal with specific topics that many people are interested in. These smoothies all have unique ingredients that focus on the targeted ailment and have shown to produce the desired results. The smoothies and their ingredients are not cures, and we are not claiming such. The ingredients used in these smoothies have worked for thousands of people and when taken in smoothie form, are easily digestible and quite delicious.

This book is written to make it easy for you to get the most out of your Vitamix blender. We've included hundreds of delicious recipes that are exclusive to the Vitamix blenders and their owners. We've grouped these recipes into easy to find and even easier to read categories that focus on maintaining general vitality and targeting specific health concerns.

Chapter 1: The Vitamix Blender for Smoothies

The Basics of Vitamix Blender

The name "Vita-Mix" emphasized "vita," meaning "life." The Vitamix blender is a high-performance commercial blender and a versatile machine. It is a necessity in every kitchen. Its uses are endless, and will help you with any kitchen task. Make homemade salsa in a few minutes. Sauces, soups, and nut butters are breeze to make in your Vitamix. As you will soon find out the Vitamix makes delicious smoothies, and even juices.

If you are in a hurry and have no time to make your meal, if you want to lose some weight and be healthy, or if you just want to enjoy a good glass of delicious creamy and frothy drink to cool you in a hot day, there is no better option than to mix up a good smoothie.

Smoothies or shakes are amazing ways to get your fill of good and healthy treats in an incredibly short time. And there is only one way of making amazing smoothies, and that is through an equally amazing blender.

What is in the Vitamix Blender that makes it the best blender for making you smoothies. Here are some reasons:

- **Trusted by professionals.** The Vitamix Blender is popular among professionals in the food business. Top chefs in star-rated restaurants and baristas in numerous large café chains swear by this blender, allowing them to not only cook up their famous dishes and well-known delicious drinks, but also craft new creations. Like a professional, you can also make all kinds of amazing smoothies with your own Vitamix blender,

- **Environment friendly.** Vitamix Blender is one of the most environmentally safe blenders out there in the market. First of all, it is hand assembled in its manufacturing house in Ohio, reducing the carbon footprint it generates. Also, 70% of the materials for the components are sourced locally within 250 miles of their center of operations, which is a big help to local industries and saves on fuel usage. Because of this, you do not have to be guilty in making your smoothies. You will not only be keeping yourself healthy and satisfied but the environment as well.

- **Unrivaled engineering.** When it comes to the product's engineering, no other blender can surpass the Vitamix Blender. It is made to last and handle years and years of usage, which is a result of careful and strict material selection. Each part of the blender is made up of high-quality materials and assembled meticulously together to form an effective, strong, and efficient superior blender. Moreover, each new model of the Vitamix Blender is based on meticulously done research. The best designs are selected from a series of them and prototypes are made for each design. Every prototype undergoes a number of thorough and strict tests for quality, so that what comes out into the market is the best of its kind.

- **Durable and sharp blades.** The Vitamix sports have one of the most heavy-duty blades in the world of top rated blenders. Its blade is constructed from exceptionally strong stainless-steel that can handle anything that you want to throw at them. Furthermore, it is formed in to a star-shape for more surface area coverage and spins at a speed of 39,000 rotations per minute. Imagine that! You can use any ingredients and you will still have your smoothie within seconds.

- **Exceptionally engineered container.** Another good thing about the Vitamix blender is its effectively shaped container. It does not only hold huge amounts of liquid (which is good, especially if you want to make a batch of smoothies for your friends or family), but it is also crafted in such a way that the ingredients or your smoothies are rotated efficiently, ensuring that you will get a nice and even creamy texture as a result.

- **Powerful motor.** As to the motor power of the Vitamix Blender, it absolutely does not lag behind the most popularly used blenders in the market. And with a motor with 2 horsepower, the Vitamix blender promises not only fast but also effortless blending.

- **Sturdy tamper pool.** Another good feature of the Vitamix blender is its highly durable tamper tool. With this tool, you can effectively and safely push down the contents of your smoothie that are harder to blend. But you will probably end up not having to use it that often though because the blades can easily handle all ingredients of your smoothies. But in case you do, there is no reason to worry about it getting all easily shredded up by the blades themselves because it is made up of sturdy and durable plastic material.

- **Incredible versatility.** The Vitamix blender is a multipurpose blender that can take on any food product you toss into it. It is very good in making purees and pastes out of hard and fibrous ingredients making it perfect in making restaurant-worthy dishes, which is why it is a crowd favorite among professionals. But it is not only good for commercial use, but in home use also, especially in making your smoothies and desserts.

- **Strict quality control.** Each Vitamix Blender that goes out of the manufacturing headquarters are scrupulously inspected and checked to ensure that what reaches the households and establishments are Vitamix Blenders of the highest quality and performance.

- **Simple and self-cleans.** Another good thing about the Vitamix Blenders is its simplicity, especially in cleaning. Because of the fluted design of the container, it is a bit harder to thoroughly clean its bottom part. However, it is not a problem with Vitamix Blender. By just putting in hot water and a few drops of dish washing liquid and giving the blender a few pulses, you will easily and quickly have clean container. It is just that simple.

Juicing vs Blending: What's the Difference?

While the answer to this question might be obvious to some, most people don't understand that there is, in fact, a clear difference between juicing and blending.

The easiest way to clear the confusion is to focus on one major quality in taste and consistency that differs between juices and smoothies. When juicing, the machine is extracting the water and the majority of the nutrients the produce contains -- but leaves the pulp behind. Blenders, on the other hand, smash every juicy bit and piece of the produce to create a thicker and fuller consistency (keeping the insoluble fiber that is also good for you).

This leaves only one more question on the table. Which is better for you? The answer to this question will depend on your health goals. While both are great choices, just keep a few things in mind:

- Because juice retains only soluble fiber, nutrients pass through your system much more quickly (easy digestion)

- Smoothies will keep you full longer since digesting them takes a little longer

BALANCE IN A BLENDER

People define "healthy" in a multitude of ways, so before we get started, let's clarify how this book defines a smoothie's healthiness. In this case, "healthy" means nutrient-dense and nutritionally balanced. The recipes in this book rely on the ingredients that provide the most nutrition while also containing protein, fat, fiber, and complex carbohydrates. As discussed earlier, together, these nutrients support blood sugar levels, helping you maintain consistent energy throughout the day and feel fuller longer. Let's discuss each of these nutrients and what role they play in your smoothie.

Protein: is the building block of muscles, neurotransmitters, and hormones. It takes longer for the body to digest, so it keeps you feeling full longer. Some key sources of protein you'll see in these recipes include dairy, nuts, and seeds.

Fats: provide long-burning sources of energy for the body, thereby keeping you satiated longer. Fat also decreases sugar cravings and improves hormone health and brain function. In these recipes, fats will come from avocados, dairy, nuts, seeds, and coconut.

Complex Carbohydrates: provide a quick-burning source of fuel for the body and are full of vitamins, minerals, phytochemicals, and fiber. Some examples of complex carbohydrates you'll see in these recipes include fruit, vegetables, and oats.

Fiber: helps provide satiety, feeds the good bacteria in the gut, and keeps you regular. Vegetables, fruits, nuts, and seeds provide the fiber in these recipes.

Whether you are enjoying a smoothie as a snack or meal, you can rest assured that all the recipes in this book are nutritionally balanced to help you avoid blood sugar crashes. All you need is to know how to make them properly!

Basic Operations and Benefit

The Vitamix Blender is incredibly easy to use. Always make sure that your Vitamix is on a level surface to start, and plug it in. Put your ingredients in the container, and make sure the lid is secured on top. Align the container with the centering pad on the motor base. Make sure it's aligned properly before turning on your Vitamix. Always have the Vitamix switched to variable and not high to start. Start your Vitamix at variable 1 and slowly work your way up to desired variable speed. If you are using high-speed, start at variable 1 and work your way up to 10. When you get to 10 flip the switch to high. Unplug your Vitamix when it's not in use.

1. Stronger Blades to Extract Nutrients and Pulverize Food

Most blender companies boast about how sharp their blades are, but blades dull over time. The Vitamix is different, because it uses the strongest blades instead of the sharpest blades. These blades don't get dull over time, they power through everything. The blades use aircraft-grade stainless steel that has been hardened. Each blade has been carefully crafted to precise specifications to create the perfect mix of slicing, and crushing. Food is no match for these blades! They liquefy fruits and vegetables with ease. There's never any leftover fibrous material to throw away so you get all the nutrients out of your fruits and vegetables.

You will quickly see why stronger is better when the Vitamix crushes ice, and turns nuts into nut butter quickly and easily. The strong blades create the perfect texture every time. Your smoothies will be completely smooth no matter what you put in them, and packed with all of their intended nutrients in an easily digestible form. These strong blades ensure you get every bit of nutrients out of your food. That's the power of strong over sharp. That's why the Vitamix Blender is unmatched by any other blender on the market.

2. Preset Operations

Some vitamins blenders come with pre-programmed settings. The settings make certain functions even easier than before. These programs are specifically designed to create consistent amazing food every time and make your life easier. Simply set the dial to the program setting, start the machine, and watch as it does all the work for you. It will stop on its own when it's done.

The Vitamix has five preprogrammed settings. The first is for smoothies. It gives you a perfectly blended smoothie every time by going through the optimal variable speeds and time. The other settings are for soups, pureeing, frozen desserts, and clean up.

3. Scrub No More

If your Vitamix has pre-programmable settings simply rinse out the container and fill it up half way with warm not hot water, and 1 or 2 drops of dish soap. Set the Vitamix to the clean setting, and let the Vitamix do all the work. When the Vitamix stops, rinse out the soap, and set the container on a towel or drying rack to dry.

4. Variable Speeds to Tackle Any Challenge

The Vitamix's variable speed control sets it apart from all other blenders. Most blenders allow you to choose from low, medium, and high speeds. This doesn't give you much control. The Vitamix give you speeds from 1 to 10 so you'll find the perfect speed for any job. This precision control gives you the perfect texture every time. Select low speeds for chopping vegetables and salsas. Select medium speeds for things like doughs. Select high speeds for nut butters, purées, soups, juices, and smoothies. The great part is you can select the right number and any range to get your dish as thick, thin, chunky, or smooth as you like. You've never had a blending experience like this, and you'll never want to go back to another blender again for making smoothies.

Now that you understand the basic operations of the Vitamix blender, let's dive into what smoothies actually are, the amazing benefits that a good smoothie can provide for your body and the foundation for making nutritious smoothies.

Smoothies

Smoothies are thick, creamy beverages usually blended from puréed fruits, vegetables, juices, yogurt, nuts, seeds, and/or dairy or nondairy milk. The most basic smoothie starts with two essential ingredients — a base and a liquid. From there, you can combine ingredients to your liking. Many smoothies include frozen produce or ice cubes to give the final product the cool, icy consistency of a milkshake. However, their flavor profiles vary tremendously depending on the ingredients.

The nutritional value of a smoothie can change drastically based on the specific ingredients used to make it. Smoothies made with whole-milk yogurt, for example, will have more fat than smoothies made with water or non-fat yogurt. Smoothies made with milk, yogurt, or water will have less sugar than those made with fruit juice.

Smoothie-making is its own kind of art. A smoothie must have a smooth consistency perfect for sipping—hence, the name! It needs to be the correct temperature (so you don't get brain freeze). Finally, the flavors need to be balanced and not muddied. We've all had a smoothie with way too many ingredients. Often, it comes out tasting like sludge.

It's tempting to cram more ingredients into your blender, but this isn't necessarily better for your health—or your wallet! You may not only end up spending more money but also taxing your digestive tract, overwhelming your system with nutrients that won't be absorbed anyway. The better way to do a smoothie? Focus on simple, whole-food ingredients. Fewer ingredients mean you can add intentional ingredients that will provide nutritional value and cleaner flavors, all while saving time in the kitchen. For a quick meal or snack option, a well-balanced smoothie will support your system instead of overloading it, and that means optimal health and wellness for everyone.

If you keep it simple, smoothies have numerous benefits for your health. They support gut health and a diverse microbiome by providing essential nutrients. Adding smoothies to your diet will keep your digestion running like a well-oiled machine. A smoothie a day may really keep the doctor away! Some people state smoothies are a magic drink for intake of multiple vitamins, minerals, and protein but less carbs. Some people joke about it as an adult's 'baby food.' Whatever, you call it smoothies health benefits are enormous.

Health Benefits of Smoothies

Smoothies are not only quick and fast; they also provide many health benefits. They are a tasty and healthy way to get Vitamins into our bodies. Within our bodies, smoothies help to improve your digestion, by reducing the trouble of constipation. They also help boost and strengthen the immune system which helps you stay healthy and stave off illness. Stronger bones can be improved with green leaf vegetable smoothies because green vegetables are rich in calcium and vitamin K. All these vitamins are necessary for ensuring calcium reaches your bones but not into body tissues.

Having smoothies every morning is an excellent beneficiary for your skin. Some skin clearing smoothie made of hemp seed, blueberries, avocado, coconut water, etc. are great for detoxing your body. The types of smoothie provide a considerable amount of omega 3 and 6 fatty acids that boost your skin and help to keep the skin cells younger. Having skin clearing smoothie give you glowing skin that you never had before. For sensitive skin with redness, irritation, acne or puffiness smoothies that contain flaxseed oil, raw almond butter, apple juice, and banana provided plant-based protein, potassium, calcium, fiber, and omega-3 which contain essential fatty acids that work as anti-inflammatory agents. So, you get trouble-free skin without any rash or puffiness.

Detoxing your body leaves a significant impact on your body organs, especially on your skin. Detoxing smoothies work to cleanse the liver and stomach. All you need is some fruits like banana, strawberries, blueberries, raspberries, kale leaves and fish oil. You can add some other ingredients like, spinach or any other veggies that you often like to add in your food or drink.

Vitamix smoothies can give us a steady flow of natural energy that lasts for hours. Fruit and vegetables do that, they provide healthful and reliable energy for athletes, students, homemakers, business people and everyone who simply needs more stamina. It is also worthy to note that Vitamix smoothie recipes contain a great deal of fruits and vegetables, which are high in antioxidants and can help in the fight against free radicals. There are plenty of them and just a few of them are: blueberries, blackberries, strawberries, apples, kale, carrots and beets.

When you replace a meal with a smoothie, you can't help but to lose weight. Replacing your meals with Vitamix smoothie, gives you what your body needs in a delicious and easily digestible manner that will help you lose the pounds fast. Smoothies are frequently marketed as a weight loss tool. Research suggests they may be effective for this purpose as long as they're not causing you to exceed your daily calorie needs. While some people find smoothies an easy way to monitor food portions and stay on top of their weight loss goals, others may not feel as full when they drink their calories rather than eating them. That said, several small studies demonstrate that smoothies used as meal replacements can be as filling as solid foods, and that drinking calories instead of chewing them doesn't necessarily lead to overeating when solid foods are consumed later

Ultimately, although weight loss can be a complex process with many contributing factors, it's important to expend more calories than you take in. If a smoothie helps you offset other calories you would otherwise consume, it can be an effective weight loss tool. If you prioritize ingredients low in calories and high in protein and fiber, your smoothie may keep you full until your next meal. Whole fruit, vegetables, nut butters, and low or no-added-sugar yogurts are all excellent weight-loss-friendly ingredients.

Keep in mind that your nutritional needs and ability to lose weight vary depending on many factors, including age, activity level, medical history, and lifestyle habits.

IS DRINKING A SMOOTHIE EVERYDAY HEALTHY?

Smoothie is indeed a healthy option to get all the nutrition that you need from fruits and veggies. But does it mean it could replace the necessity of intaking whole fruits and vegetables?

When you blend all the ingredients your target is to mix all these smooth as possible over combining charge the fiber structure of the food. So, like a whole fruit smoothie does not provide the high-quality fiber that you need. But still its a good option for having fiber as long as you continue to eat whole vegetables, fruits, and nuts more or less.

So, the thing is smoothie is right for your healthy mind and body, as long as you made it from fresh ingredients and didn't forget to eat some whole fruits and milk with it or later. You can drink a smoothie in the morning and have some apple, oranges or carrots for evening snack. That will balance a lot your healthy diet. But excluding whole fruits and veggie or dairy products and only depending on a smoothie for these is not that useful that you might think of it.

Health Concerns of Smoothies

Although smoothies can contain many health-promoting nutrients, they can have negative health consequences if consumed in excess. The most significant concern is the possible high sugar content, which can contribute to development of dental caries (cavities), tooth erosion, and obesity (Blacker & Chadwick, 2013; Maurao, 2007; Mosely, 2013; Palacios et al., 2009). Fruit contains high amounts of natural sugars and acid which, can erode away the enamel of teeth if they come in contact frequently (Blacker-Chadwick, 2013; (Palacios et al., 2009). Also, smoothies are commonly created with additional sweeteners such as ice cream, honey, or sweetened yogurt that can contribute to even higher sugar content.

There is also concern that consumption of smoothies may contribute to obesity. This is because liquid (or semi-liquid) foods do not satisfy hunger and appetite as well, or as long, as solid food (Maurao et al., 2007; FloodObbagy & Rolls, 2009). By drinking calories rather than eating them, more calories will be consumed later in order to satisfy hunger (Maurao et al., 2007). Keeping this in mind, smoothies should be consumed in moderation, taking into account your caloric needs.

Another health concern is the use of smoothies in cleanses. This can be a dangerous practice due to the extremely low amount of energy consumed (usually <1000 calories) and can lead to deficiencies in essential nutrients. Its claimed purpose is to remove supposed toxins from the body, allowing for more adequate absorption of nutrients and promoting weight loss. The liver and kidneys are extraordinary organs that perform wondrous functions for the body. One of these functions is to remove actual toxins from the body, a process they can perform without the assistance of a cleanse (Amidor, 2016; Slavin-Lloyd, 2012).

Smoothies can be a great way to increase intakes of fruit and vegetables in our diet, which would have many health benefits. However, they may contain large amounts of added or natural sugars, which can contribute to dental problems and obesity. To avoid these potential negative effects, look for smoothies without added sugar, and consume them in moderation.

Despite these concerns, an important point to note is that the best thing about eating, is to consume foods with high nutrient densities. The good news is that smoothies are the easy way to get superfoods into your body. Superfoods are special foods in a category all by themselves. They are extremely high in nutrients and generally low in calories, which can improve people's mental and physical health.

Superfoods

Superfoods are foods that have a very high nutritional density. This means that they provide a substantial amount of nutrients and very few calories.

They contain a high volume of minerals, vitamins, and antioxidants. Antioxidants are natural molecules that occur in certain foods. They help neutralize free radicals in our bodies. Free radicals are natural byproducts of energy production that can wreak havoc on the body. Antioxidant molecules decrease or reverse the effects of free radicals that have close links with health problems such as heart disease, cancer, arthritis, stroke, respiratory diseases, immune deficiency, emphysema, Parkinson's disease.

Many superfoods are in our Vitamix smoothie recipes and some of them include, blueberries, kale, beets, sweet potatoes, Swiss chard, spinach, chia seeds and flax seeds, to name a few. Vitamix smoothies make it simple to get a lot of superfoods into our bodies all at once in a quick, delicious way.

Superfood Supplements

A person can incorporate these foods into a varied healthy diet when available. However, taking superfoods in supplement form is not the same as getting the nutrients from the real foods. Many supplements contain ingredients that can cause a strong biological effect on the body. Supplements might also interact with other medications. Taking supplements could result in vitamin or mineral toxicity, affect recovery after surgery, and trigger other side effects. It is advisable to always check first with a health provider before starting to use a supplement.

Studies on Superfood

Studies have demonstrated that superfoods high in antioxidants and flavonoids help prevent coronary heart disease and cancer, as well as improving immunity and decreasing inflammation. Regularly eating fruits and vegetables also has strong associations with a lower risk of many lifestyle-related health conditions and overall mortality. The nutrients they contain help promote a healthy complexion, nails, and hair and increase energy levels. They can also help maintain a healthy weight.

A few studies have shown that soy; which is a superfood may prevent age-related memory loss. Soy isoflavones might also reduce bone loss and increase bone mineral density during menopause, as well as decreasing menopausal symptoms.

Research has also found that dark chocolate (a superfood) is high in flavonoids. Flavonoid's antioxidant activity, prevent coronary heart disease and certain types of cancer, and boost the immune system. The component in chocolate specifically responsible for these benefits is cacao powder. Manufacturers derive this from cacao beans. Bear in mind that chocolate may have added ingredients, such as added sugar, that might negate these benefits.

A few studies have shown promise that resveratrol, which is present in superfoods can protect against diabetic neuropathy and retinopathy. These are conditions caused by poorly controlled diabetes where vision is severely affected. Researchers have also found resveratrol to be beneficial for treating Alzheimer's disease, relieving hot flashes and mood swings associated with menopause, and improving blood glucose control. However, large studies using human subjects are still needed to confirm these findings.

How to Get Started

Whether you are completely new to the world of Smoothies or just learning to explore new areas, the following sections of the book will help you to get a better understanding of the whole process of Smoothie making and help you to make the best Smoothies possible.

That being said, the first thing that you should know about Smoothie making are the components that you need to have in every drink.

So, whether you are only making your Smoothie for a quick snack or breakfast, always try to incorporate the following components:

- Liquid
- Fat
- Protein
- Fiber

Fat, Protein and Fiber will help you to enhance the power of your Smoothie to keep you energized throughout the day, and it will help you to stay full and satisfied.

On the other hand, it will also provide you with all the valuable macronutrients that you may need. Just in case you are wondering, fruits, nuts, vegetables, seeds are all amazing sources of fiber, protein, and fat. Additional sources of protein include protein powders, beans and also certain vegetables. You can also find good healthy fats in oils, such as coconut oil, flax, hemp, chia or even olive oil, as well as ghee, nut/seed kinds of milk.

And lastly, we come to liquid. This is the base of your Smoothie that will help you to blend your smoothie easily and aid in digestion, circulation, hydration, skin health and even nutrient absorption, all while flushing out your body and detoxing it.

Water is possibly the cheapest and most convenient option when it comes to the liquid base, but you can always opt for coconut water, seed/nut milk or even 100% fruit juice.

Awesome Tips for Preparing Smoothies

While Smoothies are extremely easy and quick to prepare, sometimes, even if you have the best intention, luck does not stay with you and as a result, Smoothies do end up being unsavory. Or perhaps just simply due to lack of time, you aren't able to make one.

There are certain tips and tricks for situations such as these that will allow you to batch prep the ingredients for your Smoothies beforehand so that you are able to make your Smoothie in seconds after you wake up in the morning.

A good prep pathway includes:

- Make sure to properly wash, prep and measure out your ingredients before making smoothies.

- Make sure to add ingredients in a baggie jar, seal and label them with smoothie name.

- Once you are ready to sip, pour the liquid into a blender and dump all the contents of your bag into the blender and blend well.

The number of smoothie kits that you create will largely depend on the free space that you have in your freezer. But you can create at least 5 smoothie kits for your 4 days of the week, which should be a good place to start.

Another option is to fully blend your smoothie, make it and then just freeze it into cubes

HEARTY BLENDING TIPS

Every chef or expert have their own method of creating the best Smoothie! But that doesn't mean there can't be a generalized method of creating an awesome Smoothie, right?

If you are a complete beginner, just follow the steps below to get the best Smoothie ever!

- First, add the liquid base

- Then add your herbs, veggies, greens

- Next, comes the fruit

- After that, add your nuts, seeds, butter, yogurt, etc.

- Then add spices and powders if using

This would be a good pathway to follow. However, there might be situations where you might need to add spices and powders after the liquid. For example, when you are using protein powder, it may not fully dissolve if it's added on top everything.

No matter what blender you use, it is always advisable to start off slow and then slowly keep increasing the speed as you progress. If you go from "off" mode to "High" mode right away, then your ingredients will just likely fly around the blender and get stuck underneath.

Some people like to add ice to their Smoothies; you may do that if you want but be aware that it might water down the taste and balancing it out might be a little bit difficult.

As you keep practicing, you will eventually learn how to balance out the ingredients of your Smoothie and come out with the best possible flavor.

Common Smoothie Problems and Solutions

Even though the art of making Smoothies is so simple at its core, it is perfectly natural for individuals to face some sort of pitfalls, especially when you are working with limited time and ingredients. The Smoothie might end up being a bit slimy, chalky or even too slippery.

- **Too Sour Smoothie:** When you are facing this problem, try to add a bit of natural sweetener to your Smoothie, such as honey, maple syrup, coconut sugar, dates, raisins, stevia. Try to start off with about ½ teaspoon, then add more as needed. A quarter of a banana sometimes helps too.

- **Too Sweet Smoothie:** Try to add some freshly squeezed lemon or lime juice. For future reference, try to scale back on sweet fruits, add them in smaller amounts and add more if needed later.

- **Too Thin Smoothie:** If you face this situation, add frozen fruit, avocado, chia seeds, flaxseeds, cooked pumpkin, frozen cauliflower, yogurt, nut butter, smoothie cubes from leftover smoothies and so on.

- **Too Thick Smoothie:** If you see that your Smoothie is too thick, a good idea is to thin it with water, non-dairy milk, 100% juice. Add a little bit at a time, making sure that you don't overshoot and end up with a smoothie that's just too thin! Another good alternative is to add fresh fruit, instead of frozen. Fruits with high water content, such as grapes, cucumber, oranges, melon are good options.

- **Too Chunky Smoothie:** If you find that your Smoothie is chunky, then a good option is to cut your vegetables into smaller pieces so that they can blend well. Try blending your greens with liquid first. However, while doing this, make sure that you start off at a low speed and eventually increase to a higher speed. Also, whenever blending, make sure that you stop blender at intervals. If you see that your ingredients are getting stuck, simply stir the mixture, and add more liquid if needed.

- **Too Stringy Smoothie:** If you find that your Smoothie is too stringy, this might be because some vegetables, such as celery, ginger, and stems of greens do not blend properly. This might be because your blender is not strong enough. If that's the case, try to eliminate your unblended bits and blend the stringier parts with water first, strain and then finally process them with the remaining ingredients.

- **Smoothie Feels Tasteless :** If you find that your Smoothie is tasteless, you should keep in mind that the taste palette of every individual varies from one person to the next. However, it is good practice to always get the highest quality ingredients and the freshest as possible. Seasonal fruits and vegetables are the best options to go with. Another good idea is to add a bit of salt as it greatly helps to improve the flavor.

Tips to Save Time and Money

Aren't we all looking to save a minute or a dollar? Read the tips below to keep your smoothie-making fast and affordable, without sacrificing health or taste.

- **Keep on Hand:** Make smoothies a daily habit by keeping the basic ingredients in your refrigerator and pantry.

- **Minimize Cleanup:** Don't stress over having perfect measurements for your smoothies. Once you get the hang of how much of each ingredient should go in your recipe, skip the measuring cups and eyeball your measurements.

- **Prep Ahead:** Pre-portion what you need for your smoothie by tossing your fruit, vegetables, and powders in a freezer-safe bag. Store the bag in the freezer, then when you're ready to blend, simply add liquid and go!

- **Wash and Freeze:** Leafy greens can be washed, dried, and frozen to keep them fresh longer.

- **Double It:** To minimize the amount of time you're blending, double a batch of your smoothie. Simply add a lid and save in the refrigerator for the next day. Your smoothie will have the best nutrition within 24 hours. Just give it a quick blend before drinking.

- **Freeze Creatively:** Use ice cube trays to freeze dairy; chopped produce such as herbs, greens, and fruit; and other ingredients that are about to expire or spoil.

- **Refrigerate It:** Nuts, seeds, and their butters last longer and retain more of their nutrients when refrigerated.

- **Buy Frozen:** Opt for frozen produce when available. Frozen fruits and vegetables are picked at the peak of ripeness, will be more nutrient-dense, and will last longer. Plus, they provide a thick texture to smoothies, eliminating the need for ice, which waters down your smoothies.

- **Shop Seasonally:** When shopping for fresh produce, choose in-season fruits and vegetables to save money.

- **Catch the Sales:** Whenever you see fruits and vegetables on sale, stock up. Then, just wash, portion, and freeze for future use.

Chapter 2: Breakfast Smoothies

Nectarine and Orange Yoghurt

Prep time: 10 minutes | Cook time: 0 minutes | Serves 2

1 nectarine, diced and frozen
1 orange, peeled
1 cup diced golden

beets, frozen
1 cup full-fat plain yogurt
1½ cups coconut milk

1. Put the nectarine, orange, beets, yogurt, and coconut milk in a blender.
2. Blend on high speed until smooth.
3. Divide evenly between 2 cups and enjoy!

Per Serving
Calories: 504 | Fat:40g | Protein: 10g | Carbohydrates: 33g | Fiber: 5g | Sugar: 22g| Sodium: 132mg

Papaya and Pineapple with Yoghurt

Prep time: 10 minutes | Cook time: 0 minutes | Serves 2

½ cup pineapple chunks
1 papaya, cut into chunks
1 cup fat-free plain

yogurt
1 teaspoon coconut extract
1 teaspoon flaxseed
½ cup crushed ice

1. Add all the listed ingredients to a blender
2. Blend on medium until smooth
3. Serve chilled and enjoy!

Per Serving
Calories: 250 | Fat:22g | Protein: 3g | Carbohydrates: 13 g | Fiber: 4g | Sugar: 29g| Sodium: 112mg

Avocado with Kale and Coconut Milk

Prep time: 10 minutes | Cook time: 0 minutes | Serves 2

2 cups chopped kale
1 avocado, peeled and pitted
1 cup frozen grapes

3 tablespoons hulled hemp seeds
1 cup coconut milk
½ cup water

1. Put the kale, avocado, grapes, hemp seeds, coconut milk, and water in a blender.
2. Blend on high speed until smooth.

3. Divide evenly between 2 cups and enjoy!

Per Serving
Calories: 554 | Fat:46g | Protein: 12g | Carbohydrates: 33 g | Fiber: 11g | Sugar: 9g| Sodium: 76mg

Kale with Milk Yoghurt

Prep time: 10 minutes | Cook time: 0 minutes | Serves 1

1 cup baby kale greens
1 cup whole milk yogurt
1 tablespoon MCT oil

1 tablespoon sunflower seeds
1 cup of water
1 pack stevia

1. Add listed ingredients to a blender
2. Blend until smooth and get a creamy texture
3. Serve chilled and enjoy!

Per Serving
Calories: 329 | Fat:26g | Protein: 11g | Carbohydrates: 15 g | Fiber: 16g | Sugar: 16g| Sodium: 1,521mg

Vanilla Milk with Blueberries

Prep time: 10 minutes | Cook time: 0 minutes | Serves 2

4 cup leafy greens, kale and spinach
1 cup unsweetened hemp milk, vanilla
½ cup frozen blueberries, mixed

1 ½ tablespoons coconut oil, unrefined
1 tablespoon flaxseed
1 tablespoon almond butter
1 cup of water

1. Add all the listed ingredients into your blender
2. Blend until smooth
3. Serve chilled and enjoy!

Per Serving
Calories: 250 | Fat:20g | Protein: 7g | Carbohydrates: 10 g | Fiber: 3g | Sugar: 9g| Sodium: 107mg

Lemony Avocado Yoghurt

Prep time: 10 minutes | Cook time: 0 minutes | Serves 2

2 cups frozen blueberries
1 lemon, peeled
1 avocado, peeled and pitted

1½ cups full-fat plain yogurt
2 scoops protein powder
¾ cup water

1. Put the blueberries, lemon, avocado, yogurt, protein powder, and water in a blender.
2. Blend on high speed until smooth.
3. Divide evenly between 2 cups and enjoy!

Per Serving
Calories: 424 | Fat:23g | Protein: 22g | Carbohydrates: 40g | Fiber: 12g | Sugar: 23g| Sodium: 116mg

Avocado with Pineapple Smoothie

Prep time: 10 minutes | Cook time: 0 minutes | Serves 2

1 cup frozen pineapple chunks
1 orange, peeled
1 red bell pepper, chopped

1 avocado, diced and frozen
½ cup walnuts
1½ cups water

1. Put the pineapple, orange, bell pepper, avocado, walnuts, and water in a blender.
2. Blend on high speed until smooth.
3. Divide evenly between 2 cups and enjoy!

Per Serving
Calories: 451 | Fat:34g | Protein: 8g | Carbohydrates: 37g | Fiber: 10g | Sugar: 7g| Sodium: 176mg

Almond and Peach Oat

Prep time: 10 minutes | Cook time: 0 minutes | Serves 2

½ cup diced cantaloupe
½ cup frozen sliced peaches
1 cup rolled oats

1 cup full-fat plain Greek yogurt
1½ cups unsweetened almond milk

1. Put the cantaloupe, peaches, oats, yogurt, and almond milk in a blender.
2. Blend on high speed until smooth.
3. Divide evenly between 2 cups and enjoy!

Per Serving
Calories: 466 | Fat:14g | Protein: 25g | Carbohydrates: 60g | Fiber: 10g | Sugar: 7g| Sodium: 176mg

Coconut Milk and Egg Smoothie

Prep time: 5 minutes | Cook time: 0 minutes | Serves 1

1-ounce egg substitute dry powder
½ cup coconut milk, unsweetened

4 tablespoons chia seeds
½ cup organic whole milk kefir, plain

1. Add all the listed ingredients to a blender
2. Blend on high until smooth and creamy
3. Enjoy your smoothie!

Per Serving
Calories: 266 | Fat:17g | Protein: 22g | Carbohydrates: 7 g | Fiber: 6g | Sugar: 9g| Sodium: 430mg

Almond-Chia Smoothie Bowl

Prep time: 10 minutes | Cook time: 0 minutes | Serves 2

2 pears, diced and frozen
2 tablespoons chia seeds
½ teaspoon ground

cardamom
2 tablespoons almond butter
1 cup coconut milk
½ cup water

1. Put the pears, chia seeds, cardamom, almond butter, coconut milk, and water in a blender.
2. Blend on high speed until smooth.
3. Divide evenly between 2 bowls and enjoy!

Per Serving
Calories: 461 | Fat:2g | Protein: 8g | Carbohydrates: 27g | Fiber: 11g | Sugar: 9g| Sodium: 20mg

Cocoa Mocha Milk Shake

Prep time: 10 minutes | Cook time: 0 minutes | Serves 1

1 cup brewed coffee, chilled
1 cup whole milk
2 tablespoons cocoa powder
1 tablespoon coconut oil
2 packs stevia

1. Add listed ingredients to a blender
2. Blend until smooth
3. Serve chilled and enjoy!

Per Serving
Calories: 293 | Fat:23g | Protein: 10g | Carbohydrates: 19 g | Fiber: 8g | Sugar: 15g| Sodium: 982mg

Milky Strawberry Hemp

Prep time: 10 minutes | Cook time: 0 minutes | Serves 2

1 cup chopped red beets
1½ cups frozen strawberries
3 tablespoons hulled hemp seeds
1 avocado, peeled and pitted
1 cup coconut milk
1 cup water

1. Put the beets, strawberries, hemp seeds, avocado, coconut milk, and water in a blender.
2. Blend on high speed until smooth.
3. Divide evenly between 2 cups and enjoy!

Per Serving
Calories: 534 | Fat:46g | Protein: 11g | Carbohydrates: 28g | Fiber: 11g | Sugar: 11g| Sodium: 76mg

Overnight Almond Oats Smoothie

Prep time: 10 minutes | Cook time: 0 minutes | Serves 2

1 cup rolled oats
1½ cups unsweetened almond milk, divided
2 pears, diced and frozen
1 banana, halved and frozen
¼ teaspoon ground nutmeg

1. The night before, add the oats and 1 cup of the almond milk to a blender jar. With a spoon or spatula, give it a quick stir to combine.

2. Cover the blender jar and put it in the refrigerator overnight, or for at least 3 hours.
3. When you're ready to make the smoothie, put the pears, banana, nutmeg, and remaining ½ cup of almond milk in the blender.
4. Blend on high speed until smooth, adding more milk if necessary.
5. Divide evenly between 2 cups and enjoy!

Per Serving
Calories: 433 | Fat:8g | Protein: 15g | Carbohydrates: 79g | Fiber: 15g | Sugar: 16g| Sodium: 122mg

Apple and Milky Raisin Oat

Prep time: 10 minutes | Cook time: 0 minutes | Serves 2

1 red apple, chopped and frozen
1 teaspoon ground cinnamon
½ cup seedless raisins
1 cup rolled oats
2 cups whole milk

1. Put the apple, cinnamon, raisins, oats, and milk in a blender.
2. Blend on high speed until smooth.
3. Divide evenly between 2 cups and enjoy!

Per Serving
Calories: 547 | Fat:13g | Protein: 21g | Carbohydrates: 96g | Fiber: 11g | Sugar: 32g| Sodium: 102mg

Coconut Flakes with Pineapple

Prep time: 10 minutes | Cook time: 0 minutes | Serves 2

3 cups fresh pineapple
2 tablespoons coconut, unsweetened flakes
2 cups spinach, fresh
1½ cups of almond milk
½ cup of coconut water

1. Add all the listed ingredients to a blender
2. Blend on high until you have a smooth and creamy texture
3. Serve chilled and enjoy!

Per Serving
Calories: 161 | Fat:13g | Protein: 3g | Carbohydrates: 26 g | Fiber: 10g | Sugar: 7g| Sodium: 465mg

Milky Chia Oat

Prep time: 10 minutes | Cook time: 0 minutes | Serves 2

2 bananas, halved and frozen	yogurt
¼ cup shredded coconut	½ cup rolled oats
1 cup coconut milk	2 tablespoons chia seeds
	1½ cups water

1. Put the bananas, coconut, yogurt, oats, chia seeds, and water in a blender. Blend on high speed until smooth.
2. Divide evenly between 2 cups and enjoy!

Per Serving
Calories: 501 | Fat:18g | Protein: 12g | Carbohydrates: 74g | Fiber: 14g | Sugar: 20g| Sodium: 36mg

Chia Cherry Yoghurt

Prep time: 10 minutes | Cook time: 0 minutes | Serves 2

1 cup frozen pitted cherries	2 tablespoons chia seeds
1½ cups frozen mixed berries	2 cups full-fat plain yogurt
1 avocado, peeled and pitted	½ cup water

1. Put the cherries, berries, avocado, chia seeds, yogurt, and water in a blender.
2. Blend on high speed until smooth.
3. Divide evenly between 2 cups and enjoy!

Per Serving
Calories: 427 | Fat:25g | Protein: 14g | Carbohydrates: 43g | Fiber: 15g | Sugar: 15g| Sodium: 123mg

Cheesy Almond Milk with Avocado

Prep time: 10 minutes | Cook time: 0 minutes | Serves 2

2 plums, diced and frozen	and pitted
1 cup frozen blackberries	1½ cups full-fat cottage cheese
1 avocado, peeled	1½ cups unsweetened almond milk

1. Put the plums, blackberries, avocado, cottage cheese, and almond milk in a blender. Blend on high speed until smooth.
2. Divide evenly between 2 cups and enjoy!

Per Serving
Calories: 144 | Fat:25g | Protein: 23g | Carbohydrates: 29 g | Fiber: 12g | Sugar: 15g| Sodium: 742mg

Oats with Cashew Butter

Prep time: 10 minutes | Cook time: 0 minutes | Serves 2

1 cup frozen mango chunks	2 tablespoons cashew butter
½ cup rolled oats	2 cups unsweetened almond milk
1 cup full-fat plain Greek yogurt	

1. Put the mango, oats, yogurt, cashew butter, and almond milk in a blender.
2. Blend on high speed until smooth.
3. Divide evenly between 2 cups and enjoy!

Per Serving
Calories: 441 | Fat:19g | Protein: 21g | Carbohydrates: 45 g| Fiber: 7g | Sugar: 12g| Sodium:212g

Cantaloupe Berry Oat

Prep time: 10 minutes | Cook time: 0 minutes | Serves 2

½ cup diced cantaloupe, frozen	1 avocado, peeled and pitted
1 cup frozen blackberries	2 cups unsweetened almond milk
1 cup rolled oats	

1. Put the cantaloupe, blackberries, oats, avocado, and almond milk in a blender.
2. Blend on high speed until smooth.
3. Divide evenly between 2 cups and enjoy!

Per Serving
Calories: 544 | Fat:7g | Protein: 17g | Carbohydrates: 72g | Fiber: 20g | Sugar: 7g| Sodium: 176mg

Banana Flaxseed Oat with Yoghurt

Prep time: 10 minutes | Cook time: 0 minutes | Serves 2

2 oranges, peeled
1 banana, halved and frozen
½ cup rolled oats
2 tablespoons ground

flaxseed
1 cup coconut milk yogurt
1 cup water

1. Put the oranges, banana, oats, flaxseed, yogurt, and water in a blender.
2. Blend on high speed until smooth.
3. Divide evenly between 2 cups and enjoy!

Per Serving
Calories: 410 | Fat:12g | Protein: 11g | Carbohydrates: 67g | Fiber: 11g | Sugar: 11g| Sodium: 5mg

Yoghurt with Pomegranate-Raspberry

Prep time: 10 minutes | Cook time: 0 minutes | Serves 2

1 cup frozen raspberries
1 cup pomegranate seeds
1 cup full-fat plain

yogurt
¼ cup sunflower seeds
1 cup coconut milk
½ cup water

1. Put the raspberries, pomegranate seeds, yogurt, sunflower seeds, coconut milk, and water in a blender.
2. Blend on high speed until smooth.
3. Divide evenly between 2 cups and enjoy!

Per Serving
Calories: 504 | Fat:39g | Protein: 12g | Carbohydrates: 36g | Fiber: 9g | Sugar: 21g| Sodium: 76mg

Almond Milk and Honey Smoothie

Prep time: 10 minutes | Cook time: 0 minutes | Serves 2

2 medium bananas
4 tablespoons peanut butter, raw
1 cup almond milk

3 tablespoons cocoa powder, raw
2 tablespoons honey, raw

1. Add all the listed ingredients to a blender
2. Blend until you have a smooth and creamy texture

3. Serve chilled and enjoy!

Per Serving
Calories: 217 | Fat:3g | Protein: 3g | Carbohydrates: 42 g | Fiber: 6g | Sugar: 44g| Sodium: 538mg

Walnut and Banana Oat

Prep time: 10 minutes | Cook time: 0 minutes | Serves 2

2 bananas, halved and frozen
½ cup walnuts
½ cup rolled oats

1 tablespoon coconut oil
1½ cups unsweetened almond milk

1. Put the bananas, walnuts, oats, coconut oil, and almond milk in a blender.
2. Blend on high speed until smooth.
3. Divide evenly between 2 cups and enjoy!

Per Serving
Calories: 532 | Fat:31g | Protein: 13g | Carbohydrates: 58 g | Fiber: 12g | Sugar: 15g| Sodium: 742mg

Limey Pineapple Yoghurt

Prep time: 10 minutes | Cook time: 0 minutes | Serves 2

1½ cups frozen pineapple chunks
1 lime, peeled
½ cup raw cashews
1 avocado, peeled

and pitted
1½ cups coconut milk yogurt
1 cup water

1. Put the pineapple, lime, cashews, avocado, yogurt, and water in a blender.
2. Blend on high speed until smooth.
3. Divide evenly between 2 cups and enjoy!

Per Serving
Calories: 514 | Fat:34g | Protein: 9g | Carbohydrates: 48g | Fiber: 10g | Sugar: 12g| Sodium: 12mg

Spinach and Flaxseed Smoothie

Prep time: 10 minutes | Cook time: 0 minutes | Serves 2

½ cup pineapple
2 carrots
2 tablespoons flaxseeds

2 oranges, peeled
2 cups spinach
2 cups of water

1. Add all the listed ingredients to a blender
2. Blend until you have a smooth and creamy texture
3. Serve chilled and enjoy!

Per Serving
Calories: 151 | Fat:3g | Protein: 4g | Carbohydrates: 29 g | Fiber: 8g | Sugar: 21g| Sodium: 74mg

Almond Berry Smoothie

Prep time: 10 minutes | Cook time: 0 minutes | Serves 2

1 cup cherries
2 cups fresh kale
4 teaspoons honey

1 cup blueberries
2 cups almond milk

1. Add all the listed ingredients to a blender
2. Blend until you have a smooth and creamy texture
3. Serve chilled and enjoy!

Per Serving
Calories: 220 | Fat:3g | Protein: 4g | Carbohydrates: 48 g | Fiber: 4g | Sugar: 52g| Sodium: 124mg

Cinnamon and Honey Smoothie

Prep time: 10 minutes | Cook time: 0 minutes | Serves 4

2 cups brewed coffee, chilled
2 cups plain Greek yogurt, non-fat
2 tablespoons flaxseeds, ground
3 bananas, cut into

chunks
4 teaspoons honey
½ teaspoon nutmeg, grated
1 teaspoon cinnamon, grounded
12 ice cubes

1. Add all the listed ingredients to a blender
2. Blend until you have a smooth and creamy texture

3. Serve chilled and enjoy!

Per Serving
Calories: 356 | Fat:18g | Protein: 11g | Carbohydrates: 44 g | Fiber: 4g | Sugar: 22g| Sodium: 63mg

Milky Nut and Blueberry

Prep time: 10 minutes | Cook time: 0 minutes | Serves 2

1½ cups frozen blueberries
1 banana, halved and frozen
¼ cup walnuts

2 tablespoons ground flaxseed
1 cup coconut milk
½ cup water

1. Put the blueberries, banana, walnuts, flaxseed, coconut milk, and water in a blender.
2. Blend on high speed until smooth.
3. Divide evenly between 2 cups and enjoy!

Per Serving
Calories: 467 | Fat:37g | Protein: 7g | Carbohydrates: 34g | Fiber: 8g | Sugar: 18g| Sodium: 19mg

Banana-Almond-Chia

Prep time: 10 minutes | Cook time: 0 minutes | Serves 2

1½ cups frozen pitted cherries
¼ cup almonds
3 tablespoons chia seeds

2 bananas, halved and frozen
1½ cups plain kefir
½ cup water

1. Put the cherries, almonds, chia seeds, bananas, kefir, and water in a blender.
2. Blend on high speed until smooth.
3. Divide evenly between 2 cups and enjoy!

Per Serving
Calories: 457 | Fat:22g | Protein: 15g | Carbohydrates: 61g | Fiber: 15g | Sugar: 35g| Sodium: 97mg

Chapter 3: Superfood Recipes

Milky Flaxseed Superfood Smoothie

Prep time: 10 minutes | Cook time: 0 minutes | Serves 1

1 cup blueberries, frozen
1 tablespoon flaxseed, ground
Handful of spinach
¼ cup full-fat Greek yogurt
1 cup coconut milk or any kind of milk

1. Add liquid first, then softer ingredients and harder items like ice last.
2. Blend on medium and increase to high for 1 minute.
3. Repeat as necessary.

Per Serving
Calories: 474 | Fat:33g | Protein: 10g | Carbohydrates: 44g | Fiber: 10g | Sugar: 32g| Sodium: 172mg

Milk and Banana Oat Smoothie

Prep time: 10 minutes | Cook time: 0 minutes | Serves 2

2 bananas, frozen
1 medium sized golden beet
¼ cup rolled oats (optional)
1 cup unsweetened almond milk
½ cup full-fat coconut milk
½ teaspoon vanilla extract
Pinch cinnamon (optional)

1. Add liquid first, then softer ingredients and harder items like ice last.
2. Blend on medium and increase to high for 1 minute.
3. Repeat as necessary.

Per Serving
Calories: 370 | Fat:20g | Protein: 9g | Carbohydrates: 49g | Fiber: 8g | Sugar: 26g| Sodium: 95mg

Walnut with Almond Superfood Smoothie

Prep time: 10 minutes | Cook time: 0 minutes | Serves 2

2 tablespoon superfood powder
1 cup vanilla almond milk
2 cups (1 large apple) (chopped)
2 whole, pitted date
¼ teaspoon Nutmeg (ground)
½ teaspoon vanilla extract
¼ cup walnuts
¼ cup water
1½ cups ice

1. Add liquid first, then softer ingredients and harder items like ice last.
2. Blend on medium and increase to high for 1 minute.
3. Repeat as necessary.

Per Serving
Calories: 581 | Fat:23g | Protein: 11g | Carbohydrates: 88g | Fiber: 13g | Sugar: 57g| Sodium: 164mg

Citrus with Chia Seeds Smoothie

Prep time: 10 minutes | Cook time: 0 minutes | Serves 2

1½ cups freshly squeezed orange juice
¼ cup pure mangosteen juice
1 ½ cups frozen red raspberries
1½ cups frozen peach
slices
1 tablespoon chia seeds
1 tablespoon coconut oil, melted
Few pinches of cayenne pepper, to taste

1. Add liquid first, then softer ingredients and harder items like ice last.
2. Blend on medium and increase to high for 1 minute.
3. Repeat as necessary.

Per Serving
Calories: 409 | Fat:10g | Protein: 4g | Carbohydrates: 81g | Fiber: 10g | Sugar: 60g| Sodium: 10mg

Milky Superfood Berry Pudding

Prep time: 5 minutes | Cook time: 0 minutes | Serves 2

1 cup unsweetened almond/coconut milk beverage
¾ cup fresh blueberries, blackberries and

raspberries
2 tablespoon chia seeds
6 drops sugar/honey to taste

1. Add liquid first, then softer ingredients and harder items like ice last.
2. Blend on medium and increase to high for 1 minute.
3. Repeat as necessary.

Per Serving
Calories: 413 | Fat:13g | Protein: 6g | Carbohydrates: 74g | Fiber: 6g | Sugar: 67g| Sodium: 178mg

Buttered Maca Smoothie

Prep time: 10 minutes | Cook time: 0 minutes | Serves 2

¼ cup almond milk
2 frozen bananas
2 tablespoons almond butter
1 date cacao beans/

nibs
1 tablespoon coconut oil
1 tablespoon Maca

1. Add liquid first, then softer ingredients and harder items like ice last.
2. Blend on medium and increase to high for 1 minute. Repeat as necessary.

Per Serving
Calories: 297 | Fat:19g | Protein: 2g | Carbohydrates: 33g | Fiber: 4g | Sugar: 17g| Sodium: 117mg

Banana and Apple Berry Smoothie

Prep time: 10 minutes | Cook time: 0 minutes | Serves 2

2 large bananas, previously peeled, sliced, and frozen
1 heaping handful spinach (about 1½ cups)
½ of a large apple,

chopped (or 1 small)
½ cup almond milk
1 tablespoon ground flax (optional)
7 large strawberries, sliced

1. Add liquid first, then softer ingredients and harder items like ice last.
2. Blend on medium and increase to high for 1 minute.
3. Repeat as necessary.

Per Serving
Calories: 236 | Fat:3g | Protein: 8g | Carbohydrates: 52g | Fiber: 12g | Sugar: 29g| Sodium: 183mg

Spirulina Mint Superfood Smoothie

Prep time: 10 minutes | Cook time: 0 minutes | Serves 2

3 frozen bananas
2 tablespoons hemp milk or other non-dairy milk
1 tablespoon hemp seeds
½ to 1 teaspoon

spirulina powder
2 drops peppermint oil
1½ tablespoons dark chocolate chips or cocoa nibs, divided

1. Add liquid first, then softer ingredients and harder items like ice last.
2. Blend on medium and increase to high for 1 minute.
3. Repeat as necessary.

Per Serving
Calories: 555 | Fat:44g | Protein: 8g | Carbohydrates: 44g | Fiber: 7g | Sugar: 22g| Sodium: 9mg

Berry Mint Superfood Smoothie

Prep time: 10 minutes | Cook time: 0 minutes | Serves 2

1 Hass avocado
1½ cups frozen blueberries
3 strawberries
17 mint leaves
1½ cups organic

orange juice
¼ cup plain yogurt
2 tablespoons agave nectar
½ cup frozen raspberries

1. Add liquid first, then softer ingredients and harder items like ice last.
2. Blend on medium and increase to high for 1 minute.
3. Repeat as necessary.

Per Serving
Calories: 574 | Fat:20g | Protein: 28g | Carbohydrates: 87g | Fiber: 20g | Sugar: 42g| Sodium: 52mg

Milky Cinnamon and Coconut Smoothie

Prep time: 10 minutes | Cook time: 0 minutes | Serves 2

2 bananas, frozen
2 big handfuls spinach
1 cup milk
¼ teaspoon cinnamon
1 teaspoon vanilla
1 tablespoon coconut oil

1. Add liquid first, then softer ingredients and harder items like ice last.
2. Blend on medium and increase to high for 1 minute.
3. Repeat as necessary.

Per Serving
Calories: 323 | Fat:13g | Protein: 15g | Carbohydrates: 46g | Fiber: 11g | Sugar: 22g| Sodium: 322mg

Pineapple Hemp Green Smoothie

Prep time: 10 minutes | Cook time: 0 minutes | Serves 2

1 cup hemp milk
1 cup kale packed
2 cups frozen pineapple
2 kiwis, whole
½ avocado
1 banana
1 tablespoonful coconut oil
1 tablespoonful maca powder

1. Add liquid first, then softer ingredients and harder items like ice last.
2. Blend on medium and increase to high for 1 minute.
3. Repeat as necessary.

Per Serving
Calories: 502 | Fat:18g | Protein: 7g | Carbohydrates: 84g | Fiber: 8g | Sugar: 68g| Sodium: 98mg

Vegan Chocolate Superfood Smoothie

Prep time: 10 minutes | Cook time: 0 minutes | Serves 2

2 bananas
6 ice cubes
1 tablespoon coconut oil
1 tablespoon dairy free plain yogurt
1 tablespoon chia seeds
2 tablespoon hemp seeds
1 tsp camu camu powder
1 tsp cacao
¼ cup coconut milk (or unsweetened almond milk)

1. Add liquid first, then softer ingredients and harder items like ice last.
2. Blend on medium and increase to high for 1 minute.
3. Repeat as necessary.

Per Serving
Calories: 318 | Fat:21g | Protein: 5g | Carbohydrates: 33g | Fiber: 5g | Sugar: 16g| Sodium: 117mg

Superfood Chocolate Cauliflower

Prep time: 10 minutes | Cook time: 0 minutes | Serves 2

¼ cup Medjool dates, pitted (about 3–4 large fruits)
3 cups steamed cauliflower
¼ cup cacao nibs
2 tablespoon hemp
seeds
1 tablespoon cacao powder
1½ cups rice milk, original variety
2 cups coconut ice
Sweetener, to taste

1. Add liquid first, then softer ingredients and harder items like ice last.
2. Blend on medium and increase to high for 1 minute.
3. Repeat as necessary.

Per Serving
Calories: 742 | Fat:33g | Protein: 18g | Carbohydrates: 97g | Fiber: 30g | Sugar: 13g| Sodium: 854mg

Banana and Cacao Superfood Smoothie

Prep time: 10 minutes | Cook time: 0 minutes | Serves 2

¾ cup unsweetened vanilla almond milk
1 loose cup baby spinach
2 teaspoons peanut butter
½ frozen ripe banana

⅓ oz (heaping tablespoon) cacao nibs
1 cup ice
A few drops liquid Stevia (optional)

1. Add liquid first, then softer ingredients and harder items like ice last.
2. Blend on medium and increase to high for 1 minute.
3. Repeat as necessary.

Per Serving
Calories: 158 | Fat:8g | Protein: 5g | Carbohydrates: 18g | Fiber: 3g | Sugar: 13g| Sodium: 154mg

Banana and Chocolate Malt Superfood Smoothie

Prep time: 10 minutes | Cook time: 0 minutes | Serves 2

2 frozen bananas
1½ tablespoons maca root powder
1 tablespoon raw cacao powder or 2 tablespoons cocoa

powder
1 medjool date, pitted
1 teaspoon pure vanilla extract
4 tablespoons water
Cacao nibs (optional)

1. Add liquid first, then softer ingredients and harder items like ice last.
2. Blend on medium and increase to high for 1 minute.
3. Repeat as necessary.

Per Serving
Calories: 516 | Fat:22g | Protein: 8g | Carbohydrates: 75g | Fiber: 14g | Sugar: 35g| Sodium: 47mg

Blueberry with Mango Superfood Smoothie

Prep time: 10 minutes | Cook time: 0 minutes | Serves 2

200 ml organic goat or soy yogurt
1 handful frozen blueberries
1 handful frozen mango

1 tablespoon bee pollen
1 tablespoon goji berries
½ cup of raw oats or almonds

1. Add liquid first, then softer ingredients and harder items like ice last.
2. Blend on medium and increase to high for 1 minute.
3. Repeat as necessary.

Per Serving
Calories: 238 | Fat:3g | Protein: 7g | Carbohydrates: 55g | Fiber: 7g | Sugar: 29g| Sodium: 18mg

Superfood Vanilla and Pie Smoothie

Prep time: 10 minutes | Cook time: 0 minutes | Serves 2

1 frozen banana
½ cup Greek yogurt
½ teaspoon pumpkin pie spice
½ cup almond milk
2 tablespoons pure

maple syrup
¼ teaspoon vanilla
⅔ cup pumpkin puree
1 tablespoon flax seeds
1 cup ice

1. Add liquid first, then softer ingredients and harder items like ice last.
2. Blend on medium and increase to high for 1 minute.
3. Repeat as necessary.

Per Serving
Calories: 427 | Fat:23g | Protein: 20g | Carbohydrates: 42g | Fiber: 5g | Sugar: 27g| Sodium: 172mg

Superfood Spinach and Cucumber Smoothie

Prep time: 10 minutes | Cook time: 0 minutes | Serves 2

2 cups cold water
2 handfuls spinach
1 kale leaf, medium
½ long English cucumber, sliced
½ any apple, chopped
and not cored/seeded/peeled
2 tablespoon chia seeds
½ lemon, juice

1. Add liquid first, then softer ingredients and harder items like ice last.
2. Blend on medium and increase to high for 1 minute.
3. Repeat as necessary.

Per Serving
Calories: 404 | Fat:20g | Protein: 20g | Carbohydrates: 45g | Fiber: 30g | Sugar: 5g| Sodium: 284mg

Spinach and Avocado Superfood Smoothie

Prep time: 10 minutes | Cook time: 0 minutes | Serves 2

1 cup blueberries, frozen or fresh
1 cup fresh spinach leaves
1 cup almond-coconut milk
½ ripe avocado,
½ fresh ice
skinned and pitted
1 tablespoon chia seeds
¼ teaspoon cinnamon
1 tablespoon honey
1 scoop protein powder

1. Add liquid first, then softer ingredients and harder items like ice last.
2. Blend on medium and increase to high for 1 minute.
3. Repeat as necessary.

Per Serving
Calories: 580 | Fat:40g | Protein: 12g | Carbohydrates: 52g | Fiber: 10g | Sugar: 40g| Sodium: 70mg

Vanilla Berry Almond Smoothie

Prep time: 10 minutes | Cook time: 0 minutes | Serves 2

1 cup unsweetened almond milk
¼ cup fat free vanilla Greek yogurt, or a dairy free yogurt
2 heaping tablespoons protein powder
10 raw almonds
1 tablespoon golden flax seeds
½ cup blueberries
6 strawberries
Small handful of fresh spinach

1. Add liquid first, then softer ingredients and harder items like ice last.
2. Blend on medium and increase to high for 1 minute.
3. Repeat as necessary.

Per Serving
Calories: 309 | Fat:12g | Protein: 17g | Carbohydrates: 38g | Fiber: 9g | Sugar: 24g| Sodium: 244mg

Chapter 4: Healthy Diet Vitamix Recipes

Vanilla Apple Caramel

Prep time: 10 minutes | Cook time: 0 minutes | Serves 2

¼ cup caramel sauce
1 cup low fat vanilla yogurt
2 cups apple juice
1 tablespoon

cinnamon
2 tablespoons sweetener (your choice)
6 ice cubes

1. Set your Vitamix to variable 1.
2. Turn your Vitamix on, and gradually move up to variable 10, once at variable 10 switch to High.
3. Blend this delicious smoothie on high until texture is smooth, or until desired consistency is reached.

Per Serving
Calories: 313 | Fat:1g | Protein: 4g | Carbohydrates: 78g | Fiber: 4g | Sugar: 43g| Sodium: 225mg

Berry with Sweet Pea Smoothie

Prep time: 10 minutes | Cook time: 0 minutes | Serves 2

2 cups sweet peas
1 cup blueberries
1 teaspoon honey
2 bananas

2 cups almond milk
2 tablespoons chia seeds

1. Add all the listed ingredients to a blender
2. Blend until you have a smooth and creamy texture
3. Serve chilled and enjoy!

Per Serving
Calories: 202 | Fat: 4g | Protein: 7g | Carbohydrates: 38g | Fiber: 2g | Sugar: 42g| Sodium: 109mg

Nuts and Gritty Coffee Shake

Prep time: 10 minutes | Cook time: 0 minutes | Serves 1

2 cups strongly brewed coffee, chilled
1-ounce Macadamia Nuts
1 tablespoon chia

seeds
1 tablespoon MCT oil
1 to 2 packets Stevia, optional

1. Add all the listed ingredients to a blender
2. Blend on high until smooth and creamy
3. Enjoy your smoothie!

Per Serving
Calories: 395 | Fat: 39g | Protein: 5g | Carbohydrates: 11g | Fiber: 2g | Sugar: 1g| Sodium: 11mg

Milky Cafe Banana

Prep time: 10 minutes | Cook time: 0 minutes | Serves 2

1 ½ bananas
2 cups coffee (cold)
½ cup protein powder

½ cup low fat milk or soymilk
½ cup dry oats

1. Set your Vitamix to variable 1.
2. Turn your Vitamix on, and gradually move up to variable 10, once at variable 10 switch to High.
3. Blend all ingredients on high for 45 seconds, or until desired consistency is reached.

Per Serving
Calories: 244 | Fat:93g | Protein: 16g | Carbohydrates: 40g | Fiber: 4g | Sugar: 3g| Sodium: 93mg

Lemony Carrot and Veggie Spice

Prep time: 10 minutes | Cook time: 0 minutes | Serves 2

1 cup avocado
¼ cup lemon juice
14 ounces carrot juice
Dash of cayenne

pepper to taste
1½ tablespoons fresh ginger (grated)
6 ice cubes

1. Set your Vitamix to variable 1.
2. Turn your Vitamix on, and gradually move up to variable 10, once at variable 10 switch to High.
3. Blend this nutritious smoothie on high for 45 seconds, or until desired consistency is reached.

Per Serving
Calories: 252 | Fat: 15g | Protein: 4g | Carbohydrates: 29g | Fiber: 10g | Sugar: 23g| Sodium: 170mg

Milk and Lemon Strawberry

Prep time: 10 minutes | Cook time: 0 minutes | Serves 2

1 cup strawberries (fresh or frozen)
2 cups low fat milk or soymilk
10 almonds, raw
¼ cup lemon juice
1 teaspoon lemon zest
6 ice cubes

1. Set your Vitamix to variable 1.
2. Turn your Vitamix on, and gradually move up to variable 10, once at variable 10 switch to High.
3. Blend all ingredients on high for 45 seconds, or until desired consistency is reached.

Per Serving
Calories: 168 | Fat: 6g | Protein: 10g | Carbohydrates: 20g | Fiber: 2g | Sugar: 5g| Sodium: 136mg

Blueberry Ultimate Diet Smoothie

Prep time: 10 minutes | Cook time: 0 minutes | Serves 1 to 2

1 cup of soy milk (chilled if you want a cool smoothie)
½ of a medium-sized banana, sliced (if you want a cool smoothie, freeze the slices beforehand)
½ cup of blueberries (preferably fresh, but you can also use the
frozen kind)
½ tablespoon of flaxseed oil
½ tablespoon of honey or agave nectar
1 teaspoon of psyllium husks
1 cup of water (chilled if you want a cool smoothie)

1. In your Vitamix blender, throw in the frozen slices of banana, soy milk, and water. Blend well.
2. Blend in the rest of the ingredients (except the psyllium husks).
3. Finally, add the husks and give the mixture one or two more pulses to properly mix the husks.
4. Pour into a glass. Serve and drink up right away. Enjoy!

Per Serving
Calories: 283 | Fat: 8g | Protein: 5g | Carbohydrates: 31g | Fiber: 2g | Sugar: 27g| Sodium: 57mg

Cinnamon Raisin Bliss

Prep time: 10 minutes | Cook time: 0 minutes | Serves 2

2 bananas
½ cup protein powder (chocolate might be good here)
2 teaspoons cinnamon
1 cup low fat vanilla or plain yogurt
1 tablespoon honey or your choice of sweetener
1½ cups low fat milk or soymilk
¼ cup raisins
6 ice cubes

1. Set your Vitamix to variable 1.
2. Turn your Vitamix on, and gradually move up to variable 10, once at variable 10 switch to High.
3. Blend all ingredients on high for 45 seconds, or until desired consistency is reached.

Per Serving
Calories: 420 | Fat: 5g | Protein: 25g | Carbohydrates: 72g | Fiber: 5g | Sugar: 20g| Sodium: 251mg

Banana with Kale and Coconut Delight

Prep time: 10 minutes | Cook time: 0 minutes | Serves 2

1½ bananas
2 cups chopped kale
2 tablespoons flaxseed oil
¼ cup honey or
sweetener (your choice)
½ teaspoon coconut extract
6 ice cubes

1. Set your Vitamix to variable 1.
2. Turn your Vitamix on, and gradually move up to variable 10, once at variable 10 switch to High.
3. Blend this delightful smoothie on high for 45 seconds, or until desired consistency is reached.

Per Serving
Calories: 374 | Fat: 14g | Protein: 3g | Carbohydrates: 62g | Fiber: 3g | Sugar: 35g| Sodium: 53mg

Cheesy Almond and Banana Cream

Prep time: 10 minutes | Cook time: 0 minutes | Serves 2

1 cup low fat vanilla yogurt
1 ½ bananas
2 cups vanilla almond milk
½ cup low fat cottage cheese
¼ cup cream cheese (low fat is okay)
½ teaspoon cinnamon

1. Set your Vitamix to variable 1.
2. Turn your Vitamix on, and gradually move up to variable 10, once at variable 10 switch to High.
3. Blend all ingredients on high for 45 seconds, or until desired consistency is reached.

Per Serving
Calories: 397 | Fat:15g | Protein: 15g | Carbohydrates: 54g | Fiber: 4g | Sugar: 61g| Sodium: 519mg

Chia with Berry Carrot

Prep time: 10 minutes | Cook time: 0 minutes | Serves 2

1 cup frozen berries (your choice or mixed)
1 cup low fat milk or almond milk
2 cups juice or water
1½ carrots
2 tablespoons chia seeds
¼ cup protein powder

1. Set your Vitamix to variable 1.
2. Turn your Vitamix on, and gradually move up to variable 10, once at variable 10 switch to High.
3. Blend all ingredients on high for 45 seconds, or until desired consistency is reached.

Per Serving
Calories: 420 | Fat:4g | Protein: 25g | Carbohydrates: 72g | Fiber: 5g | Sugar: 47g| Sodium: 251mg

Honey and Tofu Berry

Prep time: 5 minutes | Cook time: 0 minutes | Serves 2

2 cups silken tofu
2 cups pomegranate juice
3 cups mixed berries
(fresh or frozen)
¼ cup honey or sweetener of your choice

1. Set your Vitamix to variable 1.
2. Turn your Vitamix on, and gradually move up to variable 10, once at variable 10 switch to High.
3. Blend this silky smoothie on high for 45 seconds, or until desired consistency is reached.

Per Serving
Calories: 451 | Fat:3g | Protein: 7g | Carbohydrates: 99g | Fiber: 8g | Sugar: 147g| Sodium: 42mg

Divine Chocolate Milk

Prep time: 10 minutes | Cook time: 0 minutes | Serves 2

¼ cup cocoa powder or chocolate syrup
½ cup coconut milk
6 dates (pitted)
2 cups low fat milk or
soymilk
2 tablespoons sweetener (your choice)
6 ice cubes

1. Set your Vitamix to variable 1.
2. Turn your Vitamix on, and gradually move up to variable 10, once at variable 10 switch to High.
3. Blend this decadent smoothie on high for 30 to 45 seconds, or until desired consistency is reached.

Per Serving
Calories: 335 | Fat:18g | Protein: 12g | Carbohydrates: 42g | Fiber: 7g | Sugar: 26g| Sodium: 140mg

Black Pepper and Pineapple Smoothie

Prep time: 5 minutes | Cook time: 0 minutes | Serves 2

1 cup grapefruit, chopped
½ teaspoon black pepper, freshly
ground
1 cup pineapple, ripe
A pinch of Himalayan pink salt

1. Add all the listed ingredients to a blender
2. Blend until you have a smooth and creamy texture
3. Serve chilled and enjoy!

Per Serving
Calories: 121 | Fat: 1g | Protein: 3g | Carbohydrates: 15g | Fiber: 1g | Sugar: 29g| Sodium: 3mg

Kale and Mango with Coconut Smoothie

Prep time: 10 minutes | Cook time: 0 minutes | Serves 2

3 tablespoons white beans
½ teaspoon matcha green tea powder
1 whole banana, cubed

1 cup of frozen mango, chunked
2 kale leaves, torn
2 tablespoon coconut, shredded
1 cup of water

1. Add all the listed ingredients to a blender
2. Blend on high until you have a smooth and creamy texture
3. Serve chilled and enjoy!

Per Serving
Calories: 291 | Fat: 25g | Protein: 5g | Carbohydrates: 18g | Fiber: 4g | Sugar: 12g| Sodium: 22mg

Ginger and Tangerine Smoothie

Prep time: 5 minutes | Cook time: 0 minutes | Serves 2

½ cup pomegranate
1-inch ginger root, crushed

1 cup tangerine
A pinch of Himalayan pink salt

1. Toss the pomegranate, ginger roots and tangerine into your blender
2. Add a pinch of Himalayan salt
3. Serve chilled and enjoy!

Per Serving
Calories: 121 | Fat: 6g | Protein: 4g | Carbohydrates: 20g | Fiber: 3g | Sugar: 22g| Sodium: 3mg

Chocolatey Minty Spinach

Prep time: 10 minutes | Cook time: 0 minutes | Serves 2

2 cups low fat milk or almond milk
½ cup chocolate protein powder
2 cups frozen spinach

(or 3 cups fresh spinach)
½ cup dry oats
¼ teaspoon peppermint extract

1. Set your Vitamix to variable 1.
2. Turn your Vitamix on, and gradually move up to variable 10, once at variable 10 switch to High.

3. Blend this smoothie on high for 45 seconds, or until desired consistency is reached.

Per Serving
Calories: 250 | Fat: 5g | Protein: 22g | Carbohydrates: 29g | Fiber: 3g | Sugar: 53g| Sodium: 132mg

Buttered Vanilla Yoghurt

Prep time: 10 minutes | Cook time: 0 minutes | Serves 2

¼ cup peanut butter
¼ cup jam (your choice of flavor)
6 ice cubes
½ teaspoon vanilla

extract
2½ cups low fat milk or soymilk
¼ cup low fat yogurt (plain or vanilla)

1. Set your Vitamix to variable 1.
2. Turn your Vitamix on, and gradually move up to variable 10, once at variable 10 switch to High.
3. Blend all ingredients on high for 45 seconds, or until desired consistency is reached.

Per Serving
Calories: 517 | Fat: 20g | Protein: 22g | Carbohydrates: 29g | Fiber: 3g | Sugar: 29g| Sodium: 132mg

Cinnamon Banana Pumpkin

Prep time: 10 minutes | Cook time: 0 minutes | Serves 2

1 ½ cups soymilk or low fat milk
6 kale leaves
2 tablespoons flaxseed oil

1½ bananas
½ teaspoon cinnamon
1 cup pumpkin puree (canned is fine)
6 ice cubes

1. Set your Vitamix to variable 1.
2. Turn your Vitamix on, and gradually move up to variable 10, once at variable 10 switch to High.
3. Blend this scrumptious smoothie on high for 45 seconds, or until desired consistency is reached.

Per Serving
Calories: 450 | Fat:18g | Protein: 14g | Carbohydrates: 63g | Fiber: 10g | Sugar: 1g| Sodium: 209mg

Tofu and Almond Chocolatey Date

Prep time: 10 minutes | Cook time: 0 minutes | Serves 2

1 cup pitted dates
½ cup almonds
½ cup cocoa or chocolate syrup

2 cups boiling water
1 cup silken tofu
6 ice cubes

1. Add the ice and tofu after you've let the other ingredients sit in the boiling water in the blender for ten minutes. This will soften them up for the blending phase.
2. Set your Vitamix to variable 1.
3. Turn your Vitamix on, and gradually move up to variable 10, once at variable 10 switch to High.
4. Blend all ingredients on high for 45 seconds, or until desired consistency is reached.

Per Serving
Calories: 462 | Fat:16g | Protein: 14g | Carbohydrates: 85g | Fiber: 17g | Sugar: 85g| Sodium: 50mg

Milk and Honey with Coconut Almond

Prep time: 10 minutes | Cook time: 0 minutes | Serves 2

1 ½ cups coconut water
1 ½ cups almond milk
2 tablespoons honey or sweetener of your choice

1 cup cubed pineapple (fresh or frozen)
¼ cup shredded coconut
½ teaspoon vanilla extract

1. Set your Vitamix to variable 1.
2. Turn your Vitamix on, and gradually move up to variable 10, once at variable 10 switch to High.
3. Blend all ingredients on high for 45 seconds, or until desired consistency is reached.

Per Serving
Calories: 501 | Fat:47g | Protein: 6g | Carbohydrates: 46g | Fiber: 8g | Sugar: 57g| Sodium: 220mg

Milky Flaxseed Spinach

Prep time: 10 minutes | Cook time: 0 minutes | Serves 2

1½ bananas
6 strawberries (frozen or fresh)
1 tablespoon flaxseed oil

¼ cup peanut butter
1 ½ cups low fat milk or soymilk
1 cup plain or vanilla low fat yogurt

1. Set your Vitamix to variable 1.
2. Turn your Vitamix on, and gradually move up to variable 10, once at variable 10 switch to High.
3. Blend all ingredients on high for 45 seconds, or until desired consistency is reached.

Per Serving
Calories: 517 | Fat: 26g | Protein: 18g | Carbohydrates: 58g | Fiber: 5g | Sugar: 17g| Sodium: 282mg

Honey and Cream Berry Shake

Prep time: 10 minutes | Cook time: 0 minutes | Serves 2

1 cup of strawberries (preferably fresh, but you can also use the frozen kind)
½ of a medium-sized banana, sliced
1/2 cup of low-fat

milk
1 to 2 tablespoon honey or agave nectar (for sweetening)
1 cup of crushed ice or 5 to 6 ice cubes

1. Combine the first three ingredients in your Vitamix Blender. Blend well.
2. Add in the ice and blend until the mixture is smooth in consistency.
3. Add in some honey or agave nectar if you want a sweeter drink.
4. Pour into a glass. Serve and drink up right away. Enjoy!

Per Serving
Calories: 254 | Fat: 10g | Protein: 5g | Carbohydrates: 39g | Fiber: 5g | Sugar: 23g| Sodium: 62mg

Banana and Green Tea

Prep time: 10 minutes | Cook time: 0 minutes | Serves 2

1½ bananas
1 honeydew melon (scooped in pieces away from rind)
1½ cups brewed green tea

2 tablespoons honey or sweetener of your choice
½ cup low fat milk or soy or almond milk

1. Set your Vitamix to variable 1.
2. Turn your Vitamix on, and gradually move up to variable 10, once at variable 10 switch to High.
3. Blend all ingredients on high for 45 seconds, or until desired consistency is reached.

Per Serving
Calories: 451 | Fat: 1g | Protein: 7g | Carbohydrates: 112g | Fiber: 8g | Sugar: 20g| Sodium: 1592mg

Milky Strawberry Smoothie Sundae

Prep time: 10 minutes | Cook time: 0 minutes | Serves 2

1 cup low fat vanilla yogurt
1½ cups low fat chocolate milk or chocolate soymilk
1½ cups strawberries

(fresh or frozen)
2 teaspoons flaxseed (ground)
½ cup chocolate or vanilla protein powder

1. Set your Vitamix to variable 1.
2. Turn your Vitamix on, and gradually move up to variable 10, once at variable 10 switch to High.
3. Blend this tasty smoothie on high for 45 seconds, or until desired consistency is reached.

Per Serving
Calories: 424 | Fat: 15g | Protein: 13g | Carbohydrates: 60g | Fiber: 5g | Sugar: 19g| Sodium: 256mg

Chocolatey Spunky Monkey

Prep time: 10 minutes | Cook time: 0 minutes | Serves 2

1½ bananas
¼ cup peanut butter
2 cups low fat chocolate milk or chocolate soymilk

6 ice cubes
3 tablespoons sweetener (your choice)

1. Set your Vitamix to variable 1.
2. Turn your Vitamix on, and gradually move up to variable 10, once at variable 10 switch to High.
3. Blend all ingredients on high until smooth, or until desired consistency is reached.

Per Serving
Calories: 358 | Fat: 17g | Protein: 17g | Carbohydrates: 43g | Fiber: 7g | Sugar: 45g| Sodium: 395mg

Chia and Banana Strawberry Peach

Prep time: 10 minutes | Cook time: 0 minutes | Serves 2

1½ bananas
1½ cups strawberries (frozen or fresh)
2 cups low fat milk or soymilk

¼ cup chia seeds
2 tablespoons honey (or your choice of sweetener)

1. Set your Vitamix to variable 1.
2. Turn your Vitamix on, and gradually move up to variable 10, once at variable 10 switch to High.
3. Blend all ingredients on high for 45 seconds, or until desired consistency is reached.

Per Serving
Calories: 299 | Fat: 4g | Protein: 11g | Carbohydrates: 59g | Fiber: 6g | Sugar: 23g| Sodium: 110mg

Watermelon and Berry Yoghurt

Prep time: 10 minutes | Cook time: 0 minutes | Serves 2

1/2 cup low fat milk or soymilk medium-sized seedless watermelon (scooped out in cubes from rind)

1 cup strawberries (frozen or fresh)
1 cup low fat yogurt
1/4 cup protein powder
6 ice cubes

1. Set your Vitamix to variable 1.
2. Turn your Vitamix on, and gradually move up to variable 10, once at variable 10 switch to High.
3. Blend all ingredients on high for 45 seconds, or until desired consistency is reached.

Per Serving
Calories: 219 | Fat: 3g | Protein: 20g | Carbohydrates: 25g | Fiber: 2g | Sugar: 23g| Sodium: 195mg

Strawberry and Ceylon Cinnamon Smoothie

Prep time: 5 minutes | Cook time: 0 minutes | Serves 2

1 cup baby spinach
½ teaspoon Ceylon cinnamon powder

½ cup strawberries, chopped

1. Add all the listed ingredients to a blender
2. Blend until you have a smooth and creamy texture
3. Serve chilled and enjoy!

Per Serving
Calories: 114 | Fat: 1g | Protein: 5g | Carbohydrates: 22g | Fiber: 1g | Sugar: 1g| Sodium: 12mg

Lemony Yoghurt and Sherbet Smoothie

Prep time: 5 minutes | Cook time: 0 minutes | Serves 1 to 2

2 cups of watermelon (seeds removed and cubed)
½ cup of lemon sherbet

½ cup non-fat Greek yoghurt
¾ cup crushed ice or 4 to 5 ice cubes

1. In your Vitamix Blender, drop in the cubed watermelons and Greek yoghurt first and blend well.
2. Add in the ice and the lemon sherbet. Blend until the mixture is smooth in consistency.
3. Pour into a glass. Serve and drink up right away. Enjoy!

Per Serving
Calories: 167 | Fat: 7g | Protein: 2g | Carbohydrates: 27g | Fiber: 3g | Sugar: 14g| Sodium: 26mg

Kiwi with Mango Smoothie

Prep time: 10 minutes | Cook time: 0 minutes | Serves 2

2 kiwis, peeled
2 mangoes, peeled, pit removed and chopped

16 ice cubes
2 bananas
4 teaspoons honey

1. Add all the listed ingredients to a blender
2. Blend until you have a smooth and creamy texture
3. Serve chilled and enjoy!

Per Serving
Calories: 198 | Fat: 1g | Protein: 3g | Carbohydrates: 0g | Fiber: 10g | Sugar: 74g| Sodium: 10mg

Spirulina Mango and Coconut Smoothie

Prep time: 5 minutes | Cook time: 0 minutes | Serves 2

1 cup coconut milk, unsweetened
½ cup spinach

1 teaspoon spirulina
1 cup of frozen mango

1. Dice the mangoes nicely
2. Add all the listed ingredients to a blender
3. Blend on medium until you have a smooth and creamy texture
4. Serve chilled and enjoy!

Per Serving
Calories: 138 | Fat: 12g | Protein: 2g | Carbohydrates: 8g | Fiber: 2g | Sugar: 18g| Sodium: 71mg

Lime with Mango Greens Smoothie

Prep time: 10 minutes | Cook time: 0 minutes | Serves 2

2 cups mango chunks, frozen
3 coconut powder, unsweetened
2 cups leafy greens

½ cup lime juice
2 cups leafy greens
2 cups pineapple chunk, frozen

1. Add all the listed ingredients to a blender
2. Blend until you have a smooth and creamy texture
3. Serve chilled and enjoy!

Per Serving
Calories: 224 | Fat: 1g | Protein: 3g | Carbohydrates: 54g | Fiber: 9g | Sugar: 83g| Sodium: 337mg

Creamy Blueberry Bliss

Prep time: 10 minutes | Cook time: 0 minutes | Serves 1

¼ cup frozen blueberries, unsweetened
16 ounces unsweetened almond milk, vanilla

4 ounces heavy cream
1 scoop vanilla whey protein
1 pack stevia

1. Add listed ingredients to a blender
2. Blend until you have a smooth and creamy texture
3. Serve chilled and enjoy!

Per Serving
Calories: 302 | Fat: 25g | Protein: 15g | Carbohydrates: 4g | Fiber: 57g | Sugar: 26g| Sodium: 158mg

Spinach and Grapefruit Smoothie

Prep time: 10 minutes | Cook time: 0 minutes | Serves 2

2 bananas green, peeled and frozen
4 cups spinach, fresh or frozen
1 cup green tea, strongly brewed
2 grapefruits, peeled and frozen

2 cups pineapple, chopped and frozen
½ cup full-fat coconut milk, canned
4 tablespoons whey protein isolate
10 ice cubes

1. Add all the listed ingredients to a blender
2. Blend until you have a smooth and creamy texture
3. Serve chilled and enjoy!

Per Serving
Calories: 164 | Fat: 1g | Protein: 4g | Carbohydrates: 36g | Fiber: 9g | Sugar: 78g| Sodium: 225mg

Stevia and Lemon Garden Smoothie

Prep time: 10 minutes | Cook time: 0 minutes | Serves 1

1 stalk fresh rosemary
1 tablespoon lemon juice, fresh
½ cup whole milk yogurt
1 cup garden greens

1 tablespoon pepitas
1 tablespoon olive oil
1 tablespoon flaxseed, ground
1 pack stevia
1½ cups of water

1. Add listed ingredients to a blender
2. Blend until you get a smooth and creamy texture
3. Serve chilled and enjoy!

Per Serving
Calories: 312 | Fat: 25g | Protein: 9g | Carbohydrates: 14g | Fiber: 4g | Sugar: 9g| Sodium: 79mg

Grape and Green Tea Smoothie

Prep time: 10 minutes | Cook time: 0 minutes | Serves 4

2 large avocados, pitted and peeled
4 cups spinach
½ cup fresh mint leaves
2 cups green tea, brewed and cooled
4 stalks celery,

chopped
2 grapefruits, peeled and frozen
4 cups pineapple, chunked and frozen
¼ teaspoon ground cayenne pepper

1. Add all the listed ingredients to a blender
2. Blend until you have a smooth and creamy texture
3. Serve chilled and enjoy!

Per Serving
Calories: 155 | Fat: 1g | Protein: 6g | Carbohydrates: 8g | Fiber: 11g | Sugar: 45g| Sodium: 51mg

Ginger and Strawberry Deluxe

Prep time: 10 minutes | Cook time: 0 minutes | Serves 2

2 cups of coconut water
½ cup strawberries or blueberries, organic

Half banana
½ inch ginger
Juice of 2 grapefruits

1. Add listed ingredients to a blender
2. Blend until you have a smooth and creamy texture
3. Serve chilled and enjoy!

Per Serving
Calories: 450 | Fat: 37g | Protein: 16g | Carbohydrates: 20g | Fiber: 4g | Sugar: 35g| Sodium: 255mg

Buttered Berry and Banana Smoothie

Prep time: 10 minutes | Cook time: 0 minutes | Serves 4

2 bananas
3 cups blueberries, frozen
2 cups almond milk

2 tablespoons almond butter
2 handfuls ice

1. Add all the listed ingredients to a blender
2. Blend until you have a smooth and creamy texture
3. Serve chilled and enjoy!

Per Serving
Calories: 352 | Fat: 27g | Protein: 4g | Carbohydrates: 41g | Fiber: 4g | Sugar: 53g| Sodium: 105mg

Almond Pumpkin Pie

Prep time: 10 minutes | Cook time: 0 minutes | Serves 1

¼ cup pumpkin (canned)
1 cup low fat milk or almond milk (unsweetened)
¼ cup water
1 teaspoon flaxseed

¼ teaspoon cinnamon powder
2 tablespoon honey
2 drops vanilla extract
1 cup crushed ice or 5 to 6 ice cubes

1. Combine the pumpkin, milk, and water into your Vitamix Blender. Blend well.
2. Drop in the ice and blend until the mixture is smooth in consistency.

3. Add in the flaxseed, cinnamon powder, honey, and vanilla and give the mixture a few more pulses to properly mix the added ingredients.
4. Pour into a glass. Serve and drink up right away. Enjoy!

Per Serving
Calories: 767 | Fat: 34g | Protein: 20g | Carbohydrates: 104g | Fiber: 10g | Sugar: 78g| Sodium: 275mg

Stevia Strawberry Hemp and Spinach Delight

Prep time: 10 minutes | Cook time: 0 minutes | Serves 1

½ cup strawberries, chopped
½ cup whole milk yogurt
1 tablespoon MCT oil
1 tablespoon hemp

seed
1 tablespoon flaxseed, ground
1 ½ cups of water
1 cup spinach
1 pack stevia

1. Add listed ingredients to a blender
2. Blend until you get a smooth and creamy texture
3. Serve chilled and enjoy!

Per Serving
Calories: 334 | Fat: 26g | Protein: 10g | Carbohydrates: 14g | Fiber: 6g | Sugar: 10g| Sodium: 92mg

Fruity Flax Seeds Smoothie

Prep time: 5 minutes | Cook time: 0 minutes | Serves 1

2 peaches, chopped
1 tablespoon flaxseeds, ground

½ cup of passion fruit
A pinch of Himalayan pink salt

1. Add all the listed ingredients to a blender
2. Blend until you have a smooth and creamy texture
3. Serve chilled and enjoy!

Per Serving
Calories: 114 | Fat: 1g | Protein: 5g | Carbohydrates: 22g | Fiber: 8g | Sugar: 43g| Sodium: 321mg

Berry Spinach and Apple Pie Smoothie

Prep time: 10 minutes | Cook time: 0 minutes | Serves 2

2 apples, cored and peeled
¼ teaspoon nutmeg
½ teaspoon cinnamon
½ cup blueberries
2 cups spinach, raw
2 cups of water
2 teaspoons vanilla extract

1. Add listed ingredients to a blender
2. Blend until you have a smooth and creamy texture
3. Serve chilled and enjoy!

Per Serving
Calories: 82 | Fat: 0g | Protein: 1g | Carbohydrates: 19g | Fiber: 7g | Sugar: 33g | Sodium: 33mg

Banana and Limey Strawberry Smoothie

Prep time: 10 minutes | Cook time: 0 minutes | Serves 2

1 ½ ounces baby spinach
3 ounces strawberries
1 teaspoon baobab powder
1 tablespoon flaxseed
1 banana, peeled
½ lime, juiced
1 cup of coconut water
1 cup ice

1. Add all the listed ingredients to a blender
2. Blend until you have a smooth and creamy texture
3. Serve chilled and enjoy!

Per Serving
Calories: 130 | Fat: 2g | Protein: 3g | Carbohydrates: 25g | Fiber: 6g | Sugar: 13g | Sodium: 149mg

Creamy Berry Smoothie

Prep time: 5 minutes | Cook time: 0 minutes | Serves 1

½ cup mixed berries (strawberries, blueberries, raspberries, blackberries)
½ teaspoon cinnamon
2 cups of coconut milk
½ cup heavy whipping cream

1. Add all the listed ingredients to a blender
2. Blend until you have a smooth and creamy texture
3. Serve chilled and enjoy!

Per Serving
Calories: 338 | Fat: 29g | Protein: 3g | Carbohydrates: 9g | Fiber: 2g | Sugar: 30g | Sodium: 233mg

Chapter 5: Weight Loss Recipes

Vegetable Fat Burning Smoothie

Prep time: 5 minutes | Cook time: 0 minutes | Serves 1

3 broccoli florets
2 cauliflower florets
2 Pineapple Spears

Green tea (ready-to-go)

1. Add liquid first, then softer ingredients and harder items like ice or frozen fruit last.
2. Blend on medium and increase to high for 1 minute.
3. Repeat as necessary.

Per Serving
Calories: 217 | Fat: 1g | Protein: 14g | Carbohydrates: 46g | Fiber: 12g | Sugar: 21g| Sodium: 159mg

Apple with Chia Seed Smoothie

Prep time: 10 minutes | Cook time: 0 minutes | Serves 2

1 cup apple juice frozen concentrate
1½ cups frozen raspberries
1½ cup frozen mango

chunks
2 cups spinach
2 tablespoon chia seeds
Water

1. Add liquid first, then softer ingredients and harder items like ice or frozen fruit last.
2. Blend on medium and increase to high for 1 minute.
3. Repeat as necessary.

Per Serving
Calories: 330| Fat: 1g | Protein: 3g | Carbohydrates: 82g | Fiber: 11g | Sugar: 71g| Sodium: 35mg

Vanilla Cream Avocado Smoothie

Prep time: 10 minutes | Cook time: 0 minutes | Serves 2

½ an avocado
½ cup kale
1 tablespoon cacao nibs
½ cup Greek yogurt

½ cup vanilla almond milk
½ cup frozen mango
2 teaspoon honey

1. Add liquid first, then softer ingredients and harder items like ice or frozen fruit last.
2. Blend on medium and increase to high for 1 minute.
3. Repeat as necessary.

Per Serving
Calories: 71| Fat: 1g | Protein: 1g | Carbohydrates: 16g | Fiber: 1g | Sugar: 15g| Sodium: 40mg

Berry with Green Vanilla Smoothie

Prep time: 5 minutes | Cook time: 0 minutes | Serves 1

2 cups raw spinach
2 frozen medium bananas
1 cup fresh, whole

strawberries
1 cup unsweetened vanilla almond milk

1. Add liquid first, then softer ingredients and harder items like ice or frozen fruit last.
2. Blend on medium and increase to high for 1 minute.
3. Repeat as necessary.

Per Serving
Calories: 524 | Fat: 8g | Protein: 14g | Carbohydrates: 107g | Fiber: 10g | Sugar: 76g| Sodium: 267mg

Orange and Red Banana with Yoghurt

Prep time: 10 minutes | Cook time: 0 minutes | Serves 2

6 ice cubes
½ cup apple, orange or juice of your choice
1 ½ bananas

1 ½ cups strawberries
1 sliced orange
1 cup low fat plain or vanilla yogurt

1. Set your Vitamix to variable 1.
2. Turn your Vitamix on, and gradually move up to variable 10, once at variable 10 switch to High.
3. Blend this terrific smoothie on high for 45 seconds, or until desired consistency is reached.

Per Serving
Calories: 272| Fat: 2g | Protein: 10g | Carbohydrates: 54g | Fiber: 7g | Sugar: 34g| Sodium: 110mg

Spinach and Creamy Banana Green Smoothie

Prep time: 10 minutes | Cook time: 0 minutes | Serves 1

1 banana
1 avocado
2 cups(450g) spinach

1 green apple
1 cup (240 g) Greek yogurt

1. Add liquid first, then softer ingredients and harder items like ice or frozen fruit last.
2. Blend on medium and increase to high for 1 minute.
3. Repeat as necessary.

Per Serving
Calories: 342| Fat: 19g | Protein: 8g | Carbohydrates: 41g | Fiber: 11g | Sugar: 23g| Sodium: 89mg

Avocado Green Superfood Smoothie

Prep time: 10 minutes | Cook time: 0 minutes | Serves 1

½ cup water
1½ cups freshly squeezed grapefruit juice
2 cups spinach

1 tsp spirulina
2 kiwis
1 avocado
½ cup frozen mango chunks

1. Add liquid first, then softer ingredients and harder items like ice or frozen fruit last.
2. Blend on medium and increase to high for 1 minute.
3. Repeat as necessary.

Per Serving
Calories: 266| Fat: 15g | Protein: 5g | Carbohydrates: 33g | Fiber: 8g | Sugar: 23g| Sodium: 46mg

Spinach Berries and Oats Smoothie

Prep time: 10 minutes | Cook time: 0 minutes | Serves 2

12 ounces coconut water
2 small oranges (or 1 large)
1 cup blueberries
2 cups strawberries

2 cups spinach
1 medium banana
2 cups ice (less if using frozen fruit)
½ cup rolled oats

1. Add liquid first, then softer ingredients and harder items like ice or frozen fruit last.
2. Blend on medium and increase to high for 1 minute.
3. Repeat as necessary.

Per Serving
Calories: 244| Fat: 2g | Protein: 7g | Carbohydrates: 58g | Fiber: 13g | Sugar: 34g| Sodium: 210mg

Carrot and Banana Crisp Apple Smoothie

Prep time: 10 minutes | Cook time: 0 minutes | Serves 2

1 scoop protein powder
1 cup water
1 apple, cored, seeded and quartered
1 medium orange,

peeled and quartered
1 banana, sliced
2 handfuls spinach
1 medium carrot, peeled and sliced

1. Add liquid first, then softer ingredients and harder items like ice or frozen fruit last.
2. Blend on medium and increase to high for 1 minute.
3. Repeat as necessary.

Per Serving
Calories: 97 | Fat: 1g | Protein: 7g | Carbohydrates: 15g | Fiber: 3g | Sugar: 10g| Sodium: 36mg

Lemon and Milk Avocado - Swiss Chard

Prep time: 10 minutes | Cook time: 0 minutes | Serves 2

1 cup Swiss chard (chopped)
½ avocado (sliced)
1 banana
2 tablespoons lemon juice
¼ cup fresh mint

(chopped)
1 tablespoon flaxseeds (ground)
½ cup soy milk
½ cup ice cubes
1 cup spring water

1. Set your blender to the smoothie function.
2. Blend for 30 to 45 seconds.

Per Serving
Calories: 219| Fat: 12g | Protein: 5g | Carbohydrates: 25g | Fiber: 5g | Sugar: 11g| Sodium: 83mg

Watermelon with Minty Greens Smoothie

Prep time: 10 minutes | Cook time: 0 minutes | Serves 2

1½ cups fresh watermelon chunks
Juice of one lime
1 large handful of fresh baby spinach
2 sprigs of fresh curly parsley
2 sprigs of fresh mint
½ cup frozen strawberries
1 cup frozen pineapple tidbits
½ cup frozen mango chunks
½ cup green tea or coconut water

1. Add liquid first, then softer ingredients and harder items like ice or frozen fruit last.
2. Blend on medium and increase to high for 1 minute.
3. Repeat as necessary.

Per Serving
Calories: 422| Fat: 6g | Protein: 8g | Carbohydrates: 90g | Fiber: 9g | Sugar: 71g| Sodium: 204mg

Flaxseed Green and Berry Smoothie

Prep time: 10 minutes | Cook time: 0 minutes | Serves 2

1 cup skim milk (or milk of choice)
⅓ cup plain nonfat Greek yogurt
1 frozen banana
¾ cup frozen blueberries
1 cup baby spinach
1 tablespoon flaxseed
meal
4 teaspoon maple syrup or honey
½ teaspoon vanilla extract
1 teaspoon unsweetened shredded coconut (optional)

1. Add liquid first, then softer ingredients and harder items like ice or frozen fruit last.
2. Blend on medium and increase to high for 1 minute.
3. Repeat as necessary.

Per Serving
Calories: 230| Fat: 3g | Protein: 6g | Carbohydrates: 47g | Fiber: 5g | Sugar: 36g| Sodium: 72mg

Vanilla Mixed Berry Yummy

Prep time: 10 minutes | Cook time: 0 minutes | Serves 2

1 ½ cups frozen mixed berries
½ banana
6 ice cubes
1 ½ cups plain or
vanilla low fat yogurt (or milk, low fat)
1 tablespoon sweetener (your choice)

1. Set your Vitamix to variable 1.
2. Turn your Vitamix on, and gradually move up to variable 10, once at variable 10 switch to High.
3. Blend all ingredients on high for 45 seconds, or until desired consistency is reached.

Per Serving
Calories: 229| Fat: 2g | Protein: 6g | Carbohydrates: 49g | Fiber: 5g | Sugar: 41g| Sodium: 100mg

Strawberry Sherbet Key Lime

Prep time: 10 minutes | Cook time: 0 minutes | Serves 2

⅔ cups sliced and peeled lime
1 ½ cups low fat milk or soy milk
1 ½ cups lime sherbet
⅔ cups strawberries
8 ice cubes.

1. Set your Vitamix to variable 1.
2. Turn your Vitamix on, and gradually move up to variable 10, once at variable 10 switch to High.
3. Blend all ingredients on high for 45 seconds, or until desired consistency is reached.

Per Serving
Calories: 2,939| Fat: 127g | Protein: 38g | Carbohydrates: 421g | Fiber: 2g | Sugar: 16g| Sodium: 499mg

Berry Spinach Green Smoothie

Prep time: 15 minutes | Cook time: 0 minutes | Serves 2

1 cup baby spinach or baby kale
1 cup fresh really ripe pineapple, cored and cut into chunks
½ cup plain Greek yogurt non-fat
2 teaspoons of ground cinnamon
dash of turmeric

1 to 2 teaspoons of chia seeds, flaxseed
1 small knob the size of a quarter of fresh ginger root
juice from ½ lemon
½ cup water, milk or juice
2 cups frozen blueberries

1. Add liquid first, then softer ingredients and harder items like ice or frozen fruit last.
2. Blend on medium and increase to high for 1 minute.
3. Repeat as necessary.

Per Serving
Calories: 243| Fat: 3g | Protein: 4g | Carbohydrates: 54g | Fiber: 7g | Sugar: 43g| Sodium: 43mg

Minty Orange and Mango Green Smoothie

Prep time: 10 minutes | Cook time: 0 minutes | Serves 2

1 medium mango, peeled and cubed
2 cups watermelon, cubed
1 large kale leaf or spinach
½ cup freshly

squeezed orange juice
1 cup coconut water
¼ teaspoon freshly ground black pepper
a few mint leaves

1. Add liquid first, then softer ingredients and harder items like ice or frozen fruit last.
2. Blend on medium and increase to high for 1 minute.
3. Repeat as necessary.

Per Serving
Calories: 204| Fat: 1g | Protein: 4g | Carbohydrates: 49g | Fiber: 5g | Sugar: 40g| Sodium: 135mg

Kale with Fruity Green Smoothie

Prep time: 10 minutes | Cook time: 0 minutes | Serves 1

½ large bunch of kale, stems removed
2 cups pineapple rings
1 mango

1 ripe banana (optional)
2 cups water coconut water

1. Add liquid first, then softer ingredients and harder items like ice or frozen fruit last.
2. Blend on medium and increase to high for 1 minute.
3. Repeat as necessary.

Per Serving
Calories: 338| Fat: 1g | Protein: 4g | Carbohydrates: 85g | Fiber: 6g | Sugar: 77g| Sodium: 231mg

Milky Fruit Rainbow Smoothie

Prep time: 15 minutes | Cook time: 0 minutes | Serves 1

Layer 1 Banana/almond:
130g crushed ice
2 small bananas (about 80g each with skin removed)

10 almonds
50ml semi skimmed milk

Layer 2 kale/date:
2 medjool dates, stones removed and roughly chopped
75g kale
Layer 3 blueberry
80g crushed ice

70g blueberries
50ml water
Layer 4 strawberry/ milk
80g strawberries, green bits cut off

1. Add liquid first, then softer ingredients and harder items like ice or frozen fruit last.
2. Blend on medium and increase to high for 1 minute. Repeat as necessary.

Per Serving
Calories: 267| Fat: 4g | Protein: 5g | Carbohydrates: 58g | Fiber: 8g | Sugar: 42g| Sodium: 30mg

Kale Cherry Green Smoothie

Prep time: 10 minutes | Cook time: 0 minutes | Serves 2

1 cup frozen cherries
1/2 cup frozen mango chunks
2 cups organic spinach
100% baby kale
1 banana
2 cups pomegranate-blueberry juice

1. Add liquid first, then softer ingredients and harder items like ice or frozen fruit last.
2. Blend on medium and increase to high for 1 minute.
3. Repeat as necessary.

Per Serving
Calories: 238| Fat: 1g | Protein: 2g | Carbohydrates: 58g | Fiber: 3g | Sugar: 53g| Sodium: 56mg

Milky Soy and Green Smoothie

Prep time: 10 minutes | Cook time: 0 minutes | Serves 2

A big fistful of baby spinach or baby kale (roughly 1 cup packed)
1 ripe banana, cold
¼ avocado, cold
2 cups original or vanilla soymilk
Optional: fresh mint leaves or a dash cinnamon
3 ice cubes

1. Add liquid first, then softer ingredients and harder items like ice or frozen fruit last.
2. Blend on medium and increase to high for 1 minute.
3. Repeat as necessary.

Per Serving
Calories: 265| Fat: 8g | Protein: 14g | Carbohydrates: 36g | Fiber: 9g | Sugar: 18g| Sodium: 231mg

Peach and Honey with Kale Smoothie

Prep time: 10 minutes | Cook time: 0 minutes | Serves 4

2 cups coconut milk or almond milk
2 cups blueberries (fresh or frozen)
1 cup peaches (fresh or frozen)
1 cup kale
1 small banana (fresh or frozen)
1 tablespoon chia seeds
1 tablespoon honey
1 ½ cups ice (less if using frozen fruit)

1. Add liquid first, then softer ingredients and harder items like ice or frozen fruit last.
2. Blend on medium and increase to high for 1 minute.
3. Repeat as necessary.

Per Serving
Calories: 351| Fat: 25g | Protein: 3g | Carbohydrates: 36g | Fiber: 4g | Sugar: 26g| Sodium: 23mg

Carrot Hemp Green Smoothie Bowl

Prep time: 10 minutes | Cook time: 0 minutes | Serves 2

1 handful of baby spinach leaves
1 handful of baby kale leaves
2 medium sized carrots
1 large very ripe banana
1 cup of blueberries
2 tablespoons of hemp protein powder
⅓ cup of unsweetened almond milk
1 tablespoons of almond butter

1. Add liquid first, then softer ingredients and harder items like ice or frozen fruit last.
2. Blend on medium and increase to high for 1 minute.
3. Repeat as necessary.

Per Serving
Calories: 328| Fat: 10g | Protein: 12g | Carbohydrates: 51g | Fiber: 12g | Sugar: 28g| Sodium: 358mg

Fruity Kale and Lemon Smoothie

Prep time: 10 minutes | Cook time: 0 minutes | Serves 2

8 ounces coconut water	1 cup kale
½ cup red grapes	1 carrot, cut into chunks
½ cup watermelon	Juice of ½ lemon
1 cup mango, fresh or frozen	1 date
	1 ½ cups of ice

1. Add liquid first, then softer ingredients and harder items like ice or frozen fruit last.
2. Blend on medium and increase to high for 1 minute.
3. Repeat as necessary.

Per Serving
Calories: 133| Fat: 1g | Protein: 2g | Carbohydrates: 32g | Fiber: 4g | Sugar: 26g| Sodium: 138mg

Avocado and Apple Green Goodness

Prep time: 10 minutes | Cook time: 0 minutes | Serves 2

1 green apple	5 cm piece of cucumber
2 beetroot leaves	Milk of choice (rice, almond, soy, coconut water or just water.)
3 kale leaves	
½ small avocado	
Ice cubes	
Lots of cinnamon	

1. Add liquid first, then softer ingredients and harder items like ice or frozen fruit last.
2. Blend on medium and increase to high for 1 minute.
3. Repeat as necessary.

Per Serving
Calories: 199| Fat: 8g | Protein: 5g | Carbohydrates: 27g | Fiber: 10g | Sugar: 17g| Sodium: 18mg

Cashew with Vanilla Apple Pie

Prep time: 10 minutes | Cook time: 0 minutes | Serves 2

12 ounces plain or vanilla low fat yogurt	2 sliced apples (use your favorite kind)
1 cup of low fat milk or soymilk	4 tablespoons almond or cashew butter
2 teaspoons apple pie spice	8 ice cubes

1. Set your Vitamix to variable 1.
2. Turn your Vitamix on, and gradually move up to variable 10, once at variable 10 switch to High.
3. Blend all ingredients on high for about 45 seconds, or until desired consistency is reached.

Per Serving
Calories: 520| Fat: 12g | Protein: 16g | Carbohydrates: 93g | Fiber: 7g | Sugar: 34g| Sodium: 251mg

Orange and Berry Fiesta

Prep time: 10 minutes | Cook time: 0 minutes | Serves 2

1 ½ cups orange juice	strawberries or raspberries
1 ½ cups strawberry or raspberry juice	2 tablespoons sweetener of your choice
2 peeled and very ripe avocados	
¾ cup frozen	

1. Set your Vitamix to variable 1.
2. Turn your Vitamix on, and gradually move up to variable 10, once at variable 10 switch to High.
3. Blend all ingredients on high for 45 seconds, or until desired consistency is reached.

Per Serving
Calories: 137| Fat: 1g | Protein: 2g | Carbohydrates: 35g | Fiber: 5g | Sugar: 34g| Sodium: 3mg

Tofu and Banana - Choco Split

Prep time: 10 minutes | Cook time: 0 minutes | Serves 2

¼ cup cocoa powder (or chocolate syrup)	or soy milk
1 ½ bananas	3 tablespoons sweetener (your choice)
¾ cups tofu	
1 ½ cups low fat milk	

1. Set your Vitamix to variable 1.
2. Turn your Vitamix on, and gradually move up to variable 10, once at variable 10 switch to High.
3. Blend this deliciously smoothie on high for 45 seconds, or until desired consistency is reached.

Per Serving
Calories: 246| Fat: 7g | Protein: 16g | Carbohydrates: 40g | Fiber: 8g | Sugar: 33g| Sodium: 95mg

Milky Banana and Butter Delight

Prep time: 10 minutes | Cook time: 0 minutes | Serves 2

1 banana	preferably)
1 ¼ cups low fat milk (or soy milk)	2 tablespoons protein powder
⅔ cups smooth peanut butter (low fat	8 ice cubes

1. Set your Vitamix to variable 1.
2. Turn your Vitamix on, and gradually move up to variable 10, once at variable 10 switch to High.
3. Blend all ingredients on high speed, or until desired consistency is reached.

Per Serving
Calories: 752| Fat: 47g | Protein: 50g | Carbohydrates: 42g | Fiber: 7g | Sugar: 27g| Sodium: 166mg

Honey Soy Blue Smoothie

Prep time: 10 minutes | Cook time: 0 minutes | Serves 2

⅔ cups soy protein	16 ounces water
1 large banana	1 tablespoon honey or sweetener of your choice
½ cup frozen blueberries	
1 tablespoon flaxseed oil	6 ice cubes (if desired)

1. Set your Vitamix to variable 1.
2. Turn your Vitamix on, and gradually move up to variable 10, once at variable 10 switch to High.
3. Blend all ingredients on high for 45 seconds, or until desired consistency is reached.

Per Serving
Calories: 222| Fat: 0g | Protein: 4g | Carbohydrates: 34g | Fiber: 3g | Sugar: 20g| Sodium: 71mg

Vanilla Cashew Banana

Prep time: 10 minutes | Cook time: 0 minutes | Serves 2

2 tablespoons cashew butter	(plain or vanilla)
1 ½ bananas	3 tablespoons sweetener (your choice)
1 tablespoon flaxseed oil	
1 cup low fat yogurt	1 tablespoon vanilla extract.

1. Set your Vitamix to variable 1.
2. Turn your Vitamix on, and gradually move up to variable 10, once at variable 10 switch to High.
3. Blend this scrumptious smoothie on high for 30 to 45 seconds, or until desired consistency is reached.

Per Serving
Calories: 350| Fat: 17g | Protein: 9g | Carbohydrates: 44g | Fiber: 4g | Sugar: 34g| Sodium: 64mg

Orange Yoghurt Citrus Joy

Prep time: 10 minutes | Cook time: 0 minutes | Serves 2

12 ounces citrus flavored yogurt (your choice)
2 oranges cut into pieces

1 ½ cups soymilk or low fat milk
1 ½ tablespoons flaxseed oil
8 ice cubes

1. Set your Vitamix to variable 1.
2. Turn your Vitamix on, and gradually move up to variable 10, once at variable 10 switch to High.
3. Blend all ingredients on high for 45 seconds, or until desired consistency is reached.

Per Serving
Calories: 393| Fat: 13g | Protein: 12g | Carbohydrates: 52g | Fiber: 6g | Sugar: 13g| Sodium: 207mg

Fruity Grab Bag

Prep time: 10 minutes | Cook time: 0 minutes | Serves 2

1 banana
½ cup apple slices
1 ½ oranges (peeled and sectioned)
3 tablespoons honey

(or your choice of sweetener)
8 ice cubes
1 cup low fat milk or soymilk

1. Set your Vitamix to variable 1.
2. Turn your Vitamix on, and gradually move up to variable 10, once at variable 10 switch to High.
3. Blend all ingredients on high for 45 seconds, or until desired consistency is reached.

Per Serving
Calories: 782| Fat: 17g | Protein: 34g | Carbohydrates: 126g | Fiber: 11g | Sugar: 46g| Sodium: 502mg

Pineapple and Milk Flaxseed Supreme

Prep time: 10 minutes | Cook time: 0 minutes | Serves 2

8 ounces pineapple chunks with juice (canned is fine)
1 ½ cups low fat milk or soymilk
2 tablespoons

flaxseed oil
8 ice cubes
3 tablespoons sweetener (your choice)

1. Set your Vitamix to variable 1.
2. Turn your Vitamix on, and gradually move up to variable 10, once at variable 10 switch to High.
3. Blend this tropical smoothie on high for 45 seconds, or until desired consistency is reached.

Per Serving
Calories: 263| Fat: 16g | Protein: 7g | Carbohydrates: 28g | Fiber: 3g | Sugar: 26g| Sodium: 110mg

Ginger Apple and Cucumber with Lemon

Prep time: 10 minutes | Cook time: 0 minutes | Serves 1

1 cup kale or spinach or romaine lettuce
1 apple (peeled, sliced and de-seeded)
¼ bunch parsley
½ cucumber (peeled and sliced)

1 celery stalk (chopped)
½ lemon (peeled, sliced and de-seeded)
2 teaspoons ginger (chopped)
1 cup spring water

1. Set your Vitamix to variable 1.
2. Turn your Vitamix on, and gradually move up to variable 10, once at variable 10 switch to High.
3. Blend all ingredients on high for 30 to 45 seconds, or until desired consistency is reached.

Per Serving
Calories: 187| Fat: 1g | Protein: 6g | Carbohydrates: 44g | Fiber: 9g | Sugar: 23g| Sodium: 82mg

Carrot and Apple Hot Tomato

Prep time: 10 minutes | Cook time: 0 minutes | Serves 1

½ cup apple juice
1 cup tomato juice
1 ½ cups chopped tomatoes
⅔ cups chopped carrots
⅔ cups chopped celery
⅔ teaspoons hot sauce
9 ice cubes

1. Set your Vitamix to variable 1.
2. Turn your Vitamix on, and gradually move up to variable 10, once at variable 10 switch to High.
3. Blend all ingredients on high for 45 seconds, or until desired consistency is reached.

Per Serving
Calories: 95| Fat: 1g | Protein: 3g | Carbohydrates: 22g | Fiber: 4g | Sugar: 3g| Sodium: 462mg

Limey Mango Bliss

Prep time: 10 minutes | Cook time: 0 minutes | Serves 2

1 cup mango juice (bottled is fine)
2 tablespoons sweetener (your choice)
2 tablespoons lime or lemon juice
5 ice cubes
½ cup mashed ripe avocado
½ cup plain or vanilla low fat yogurt
½ cup mangoes – cubed

1. Set your Vitamix to variable 1.
2. Turn your Vitamix on, and gradually move up to variable 10, once at variable 10 switch to High.
3. Blend this tasty smoothie on high for 45 seconds, or until desired consistency is reached.

Per Serving
Calories: 207| Fat: 8g | Protein: 3g | Carbohydrates: 38g | Fiber: 6g | Sugar: 31g| Sodium: 73mg

Berry and Melon Perfection

Prep time: 5 minutes | Cook time: 0 minutes | Serves 2

3 cups cantaloupe pieces
1 ½ cups raspberries or strawberries (frozen or fresh)
8 ice cubes
1 ½ cups chopped lettuce leaves (Romaine preferably, or to taste)

1. Set your Vitamix to variable 1.
2. Turn your Vitamix on, and gradually move up to variable 10, once at variable 10 switch to High.
3. Blend all ingredients on high for 45 seconds, or until desired consistency is reached.

Per Serving
Calories: 129| Fat: 1g | Protein: 3g | Carbohydrates: 30g | Fiber: 8g | Sugar: 30g| Sodium: 69mg

Chia Espresso with Vanilla Yoghurt

Prep time: 10 minutes | Cook time: 0 minutes | Serves 2

4 teaspoons cocoa powder
2 shots espresso
1 cup low-fat plain or vanilla yogurt
2 tablespoons chia seeds
2 tablespoons sweetener (Your choice)
6 ice cubes

1. Set your Vitamix to variable 1.
2. Turn your Vitamix on, and gradually move up to variable 10, once at variable 10 switch to High.
3. Blend this energizing smoothie on high for 45 seconds, or until desired consistency is reached.

Per Serving
Calories: 256| Fat: 12g | Protein: 14g | Carbohydrates: 24g | Fiber: 13g | Sugar: 18g| Sodium: 108mg

Milky Peach with Chia

Prep time: 10 minutes | Cook time: 0 minutes | Serves 2

1 ½ cups sliced frozen or fresh peaches
1 tablespoon chia seeds
1 ½ cups low fat or non-fat milk
4 ice cubes
3 tablespoons sweetener (your choice)

1. Set your Vitamix to variable 1.
2. Turn your Vitamix on, and gradually move up to variable 10, once at variable 10 switch to High.
3. Blend all ingredients on high for 45 seconds, or until desired consistency is reached.

Per Serving
Calories: 195| Fat: 5g | Protein: 10g | Carbohydrates: 30g | Fiber: 5g | Sugar: 17g| Sodium: 112mg

Yoghurt and Chips Raspberry Treat

Prep time: 10 minutes | Cook time: 0 minutes | Serves 2

10 ounces plain or vanilla low fat yogurt
1 cup low fat, skim milk or soymilk
½ cup dark chocolate chips
1 ½ cups raspberries (frozen or fresh)
1 ½ cups raspberry juice
6 ice cubes

1. Set your Vitamix to variable 1.
2. Turn your Vitamix on, and gradually move up to variable 10, once at variable 10 switch to High.
3. Blend all ingredients on high for 45 seconds, or until desired consistency is reached.

Per Serving
Calories: 557| Fat: 13g | Protein: 14g | Carbohydrates: 102g | Fiber: 7g | Sugar: 87g| Sodium: 223mg

Carrot and Strawberry Oatmeal

Prep time: 15 minutes | Cook time: 0 minutes | Serves 2

½ banana
¼ cup orange juice
¼ cup strawberries (frozen or fresh)
6 ounces plain or vanilla yogurt
½ cup spinach
4 baby carrots
¼ cup protein powder
1 teaspoon flaxseed oil
4 ice cubes
1 tablespoon dry oatmeal

1. Set your Vitamix to variable 1.
2. Turn your Vitamix on, and gradually move up to variable 10, once at variable 10 switch to High.
3. Blend all ingredients on high for 45 seconds, or until desired consistency is reached.

Per Serving
Calories: 206| Fat: 5g | Protein: 17g | Carbohydrates: 24g | Fiber: 2g | Sugar: 14g| Sodium: 156mg

Peachy Fruit and Yoghurt

Prep time: 10 minutes | Cook time: 0 minutes | Serves 2

2 frozen bananas
1 ½ cups peach slices (frozen or fresh)
½ cup blueberries (or strawberries)
1 cup low fat plain or vanilla yogurt
2 tablespoons protein powder
½ cup low fat milk or soymilk

1. Set your Vitamix to variable 1.
2. Turn your Vitamix on, and gradually move up to variable 10, once at variable 10 switch to High.
3. Blend all ingredients on high for 45 seconds, or until desired consistency is reached.

Per Serving
Calories: 463| Fat: 7g | Protein: 34g | Carbohydrates: 63g | Fiber: 3g | Sugar: 40g| Sodium: 388mg

Chapter 6: Anti-Aging Recipes

Vanilla Berry Anti-Aging Smoothie

Prep time: 5 minutes | Cook time: 0 minutes | Serves 1

½ cup fresh or frozen blueberries
1½ cup fresh sliced peach, with peel or frozen peaches, pits removed
About ¾ cup unsweetened vanilla almond milk, to the fill line

1. Add liquid first, then softer ingredients and harder items like ice or frozen fruit last.
2. Blend on medium and increase to high for 1 minute.
3. Repeat as necessary.

Per Serving
Calories: 399| Fat: 3g | Protein: 3g | Carbohydrates: 100g | Fiber: 8g | Sugar: 91g| Sodium: 138mg

Anti-Aging Turmeric Smoothie

Prep time: 10 minutes | Cook time: 0 minutes | Serves 2

1 cup coconut milk
½ cup frozen pineapple or mango chunks
1 fresh banana
1 tablespoon coconut oil
1 teaspoon turmeric
½ teaspoon cinnamon
½ teaspoon ginger
½ avocado

1. Add liquid first, then softer ingredients and harder items like ice or frozen fruit last.
2. Blend on medium and increase to high for 1 minute.
3. Repeat as necessary.

Per Serving
Calories: 325| Fat: 18g | Protein: 6g | Carbohydrates: 39g | Fiber: 6g | Sugar: 27g| Sodium: 58mg

Vanilla and Chocolate Berry Almond Blast

Prep time: 10 minutes | Cook time: 0 minutes | Serves 2

1 cup spinach
1 tablespoon cacao nibs
1 tablespoon almond butter
½ cup cherries,
frozen
½ cup mixed berries
1 splash vanilla
½ teaspoon Ceylon cinnamon
1 ½ cups almond milk

1. Add liquid first, then softer ingredients and harder items like ice or frozen fruit last.
2. Blend on medium and increase to high for 1 minute.
3. Repeat as necessary.

Per Serving
Calories: 297| Fat: 12g | Protein: 3g | Carbohydrates: 47g | Fiber: 3g | Sugar: 34g| Sodium: 399mg

Watermelon and Coconut Chia Smoothie

Prep time: 10 minutes | Cook time: 0 minutes | Serves 2

1 cup wild frozen blueberries, or just frozen blueberries
1 cup cubed raw red beets, peeled
1 cup cubed
watermelon
1 cup coconut water
1 teaspoon chia seeds (optional)
1 handful of basil leaves (or mint)

1. Add liquid first, then softer ingredients and harder items like ice or frozen fruit last.
2. Blend on medium and increase to high for 1 minute.
3. Repeat as necessary.

Per Serving
Calories: 160| Fat: 1g | Protein: 6g | Carbohydrates: 38g | Fiber: 8g | Sugar: 28g| Sodium: 429mg

Carrot and Turmeric Antioxidant Smoothie

Prep time: 10 minutes | Cook time: 0 minutes | Serves 2

2 tangerines, peeled	1 teaspoon turmeric
1 large organic carrot, chopped	1 teaspoon Dole milled chia seeds
½ avocado	6 ice cubes
1 cup coconut milk	

1. Add liquid first, then softer ingredients and harder items like ice or frozen fruit last.
2. Blend on medium and increase to high for 1 minute.
3. Repeat as necessary.

Per Serving
Calories: 223| Fat: 12g | Protein: 6g | Carbohydrates: 27g | Fiber: 7g | Sugar: 17g| Sodium: 73mg

Grapy Raspberry Antioxidant Smoothie

Prep time: 5 minutes | Cook time: 0 minutes | Serves 2

1 cup red seedless grapes	3 red plums, pits removed
2 handfuls spinach	½ cup raspberries

1. Add liquid first, then softer ingredients and harder items like ice or frozen fruit last.
2. Blend on medium and increase to high for 1 minute.
3. Repeat as necessary.

Per Serving
Calories: 250| Fat: 2g | Protein: 11g | Carbohydrates: 57g | Fiber: 11g | Sugar: 41g| Sodium: 285mg

Parsley and Apple Anti-Aging Smoothie

Prep time: 10 minutes | Cook time: 0 minutes | Serves 2

1 ½ cup kale cut up	(Cored)
2 Celery sticks	1 handful parsley
1 juice whole lemon	1 ½ cup coconut water
1 medium apple	

1. Add liquid first, then softer ingredients and harder items like ice or frozen fruit last.
2. Blend on medium and increase to high for 1 minute.
3. Repeat as necessary.

Per Serving
Calories: 96| Fat: 1g | Protein: 2g | Carbohydrates: 22g | Fiber: 5g | Sugar: 15g| Sodium: 209mg

Honey and Grape Goji Blast

Prep time: 10 minutes | Cook time: 0 minutes | Serves 2

1 banana	½ cup blueberries
1 tablespoon cacao	1 tablespoon honey
¼ cup Goji berries	3 ice cubes
½ cup grapes	To max line water

1. Add liquid first, then softer ingredients and harder items like ice or frozen fruit last.
2. Blend on medium and increase to high for 1 minute. Repeat as necessary.

Per Serving
Calories: 184| Fat: 1g | Protein: 2g | Carbohydrates: 47g | Fiber: 3g | Sugar: 38g| Sodium: 5mg

Yoghurt with Watermelon Smoothie

Prep time: 10 minutes | Cook time: 0 minutes | Serves 2

1½ cups watermelon (seedless or remove seeds)	cored
1 frozen banana	¾ cup fat free thick Greek yogurt
1 apple, peeled and	Agave or honey

1. Add liquid first, then softer ingredients and harder items like ice or frozen fruit last.
2. Blend on medium and increase to high for 1 minute.
3. Repeat as necessary.

Per Serving
Calories: 202| Fat: 1g | Protein: 3g | Carbohydrates: 49g | Fiber: 8g | Sugar: 29g| Sodium: 59mg

Avocado and Berry Nice

Prep time: 10 minutes | Cook time: 0 minutes | Serves 2

½ cup strawberries	2 tablespoons ground
¾ cups blueberries	flaxseed
½ avocado	1 cup ice cubes

1. Set your Vitamix to variable 1.
2. Turn your Vitamix on, and gradually move up to variable 10, once at variable 10 switch to High.
3. Blend on high 30 to 45 seconds or until desired consistency is reached.

Per Serving
Calories: 157| Fat: 11g | Protein: 2g | Carbohydrates: 16g | Fiber: 6g | Sugar: 26g| Sodium: 8mg

Chia Berry Anti-Aging Superfood

Prep time: 10 minutes | Cook time: 0 minutes | Serves 1

Water as needed	seeds
½ cup unsweetened nut milk	1 tablespoon almond butter
2 scoops vanilla whey protein	¼ cup frozen blueberries
1 tablespoon unrefined coconut oil	½ stick frozen acai puree
1 tablespoon chia	

1. Add all the listed ingredients to a blender
2. Blend until you have a smooth and creamy texture
3. Serve chilled and enjoy!

Per Serving
Calories: 162| Fat: 14g | Protein: 3g | Carbohydrates: 10g | Fiber: 4g | Sugar: 8g| Sodium: 379mg

Mango and Avocado Glowing Skin Glass

Prep time: 10 minutes | Cook time: 0 minutes | Serves 1

½ avocado, sliced	2 frozen bananas, peeled and sliced
2 cups kale	
1 cup mango, chopped	½ cup of coconut water
1 cup pineapple, chopped	1 tablespoon flax

1. Add all the listed ingredients to a blender
2. Blend until you have a smooth and creamy texture
3. Serve chilled and enjoy!

Per Serving
Calories: 430| Fat: 40g | Protein: 3g | Carbohydrates: 20g | Fiber: 14g | Sugar: 63g| Sodium: 240mg

Strawberry Green Tea with Coconut

Prep time: 10 minutes | Cook time: 0 minutes | Serves 2

2 tablespoons green tea powder	seeds
	¼ cup plain yogurt
1 ½ bananas	2 tablespoons
3 cups strawberries	sweetener (honey or
2 cups coconut water	your choice)
3 tablespoons chia	

1. Set your Vitamix to variable 1.
2. Turn your Vitamix on, and gradually move up to variable 10, once at variable 10 switch to High.
3. Blend thoroughly on high until desired consistency is reached, around 45 seconds.

Per Serving
Calories: 464| Fat: 17g | Protein: 15g | Carbohydrates: 67g | Fiber: 26g | Sugar: 38g| Sodium: 276mg

Milky Kale and Banana Delight

Prep time: 10 minutes | Cook time: 0 minutes | Serves 2

1 banana	¼ cup pitted dates
1 cup kale leaves (or collard greens or bok choy)	1 cup arugula
	1 cup milk (soy or almond milk is ok)

1. Set your Vitamix to variable 1.
2. Turn your Vitamix on, and gradually move up to variable 10, once at variable 10 switch to High.
3. Blend on high for 30 to 45 seconds or until desired consistency is reached.

Per Serving
Calories: 195| Fat: 3g | Protein: 7g | Carbohydrates: 40g | Fiber: 4g | Sugar: 25g| Sodium: 76mg

Lemony Carrot with Kale

Prep time: 10 minutes | Cook time: 0 minutes | Serves 2

2 carrots (cleaned and chopped)
2 cups kale (leaves only, no stems)
2 ½ cups coconut
water
1 ½ apples (green preferably)
¼ cup lemon juice

1. Set your Vitamix to variable 1.
2. Turn your Vitamix on, and gradually move up to variable 10, once at variable 10 switch to High.
3. Enjoy this delicious smoothie after blending well on high for about 1 minute, or until desired consistency is reached.

Per Serving
Calories: 193| Fat: 1g | Protein: 5g | Carbohydrates: 44g | Fiber: 9g | Sugar: 25g| Sodium: 393mg

Berry and Minty Coconut with Lemon

Prep time: 10 minutes | Cook time: 0 minutes | Serves 2

2 ½ cups coconut water
1 ½ cups blueberries
1 ½ cups strawberries
2 teaspoons chia
seeds
¼ cup leaves of mint
2 tablespoons lemon juice

1. Put all the ingredients in your Vitamix.
2. Set your Vitamix to variable 1.
3. Turn your Vitamix on, and gradually move up to variable 10, once at variable 10 switch to High.

Per Serving
Calories: 417| Fat: 17g | Protein: 11g | Carbohydrates: 60g | Fiber: 20g | Sugar: 53g| Sodium: 323mg

Milky Peach and Almond with Blueberry

Prep time: 5 minutes | Cook time: 0 minutes | Serves 2

2 cups low fat milk or almond or soy milk
2 cups sliced peaches
(fresh is best, then frozen, then canned)
1 cup blueberry

1. Add sweetener if desired.
2. Set your Vitamix to variable 1.

3. Turn your Vitamix on, and gradually move up to variable 10; once at variable 10, switch to High.
4. Blend smoothie on high for around 30 seconds or until desired consistency is reached.

Per Serving
Calories: 408| Fat: 10g | Protein: 11g | Carbohydrates: 70g | Fiber: 19g | Sugar: 84g| Sodium: 276mg

Kale with Pineapple and Chia Express

Prep time: 10 minutes | Cook time: 0 minutes | Serves 2

2 cups pineapple chunks
1 ½ cup mango chunks
2 cups coconut water
1 ½ cups kale (chopped)
2 tablespoons chia seeds

1. Set your Vitamix to variable 1.
2. Turn your Vitamix on, and gradually move up to variable 10, once at variable 10 switch to High.
3. Blend the smoothie for at least 35 seconds, or until desired consistency is reached on high.

Per Serving
Calories: 336| Fat: 1g | Protein: 4g | Carbohydrates: 83g | Fiber: 8g | Sugar: 75g| Sodium: 263mg

Lemon and Mint Breezy Blueberry

Prep time: 10 minutes | Cook time: 0 minutes | Serves 1

Handful of mint
1 teaspoon chia seeds
1 tablespoon lemon juice
1 cup of coconut water
1 cup strawberries
1 cup blueberries

1. Add all the listed ingredients to a blender
2. Blend until you have a smooth and creamy texture
3. Serve chilled and enjoy!

Per Serving
Calories: 169| Fat: 13g | Protein: 6g | Carbohydrates: 11g | Fiber: 10g | Sugar: 94g| Sodium: 262mg

Chia with Pineapple and Mango

Prep time: 5 minutes | Cook time: 0 minutes | Serves 2

1 ½ cups pineapple chunks
1 cup mango chunks
2 ½ cups coconut

water
2 tablespoons chia seeds

1. Set your Vitamix to variable 1.
2. Turn your Vitamix on, and gradually move up to variable 10, once at variable 10 switch to High.
3. Blend this tasty drink on high for around 50 seconds, or until desired consistency is reached.

Per Serving
Calories: 341| Fat: 10g | Protein: 10g | Carbohydrates: 54g | Fiber: 17g | Sugar: 58g| Sodium: 317mg

Pear with Ginger Pure Gold

Prep time: 10 minutes | Cook time: 0 minutes | Serves 2

½ carrot (sliced)
½ papaya (sliced)
1 orange (sliced)
½ cup pear juice

1 teaspoon sliced ginger
½ cup ice cubes

1. Set your Vitamix to variable 1.
2. Turn your Vitamix on, and gradually move up to variable 10, once at variable 10 switch to High.
3. Blend the smoothie on high for 30 to 45 seconds, or until desired consistency is reached.

Per Serving
Calories: 123| Fat: 0g | Protein: 2g | Carbohydrates: 30g | Fiber: 4g | Sugar: 9g| Sodium: 19mg

Banana and Almond Relaxing Oatmeal

Prep time: 10 minutes | Cook time: 0 minutes | Serves 2

¾ cups dried oatmeal
¾ cups raw almonds (chopped finely)
1 ½ bananas
2 ½ cups coconut

water
3 tablespoons sweetener (your choice, though honey is preferred)

1. Set your Vitamix to variable 1.
2. Turn your Vitamix on, and gradually move up to variable 10, once at variable 10 switch to High.
3. Blend this relaxing beverage on high for about 45 seconds or until desired consistency is reached.

Per Serving
Calories: 924| Fat: 41g | Protein: 0g | Carbohydrates: 119g | Fiber: 26g | Sugar: 47g| Sodium: 636mg

Lemon and Milk Sunflower with Spinach

Prep time: 10 minutes | Cook time: 0 minutes | Serves 1

1 cup unsweetened almond milk
2 tablespoons lemon juice
2 tablespoons avocado, peeled and

pit removed
1 tablespoon sunflower seeds
½ medium banana, ripe
1 cup packed spinach

1. Add all the listed ingredients to a blender
2. Blend until you have a smooth and creamy texture
3. Serve chilled and enjoy!

Per Serving
Calories: 401| Fat: 42g | Protein: 2g | Carbohydrates: 4g | Fiber: 30g | Sugar: 23g| Sodium: 158mg

Coconut Delight with Anti-Aging Turmeric

Prep time: 10 minutes | Cook time: 0 minutes | Serves 1

1 tablespoon coconut oil
2 teaspoons chia seeds
1 teaspoon ground

turmeric
1 banana, frozen
½ cup pineapple, diced
1 cup of coconut milk

1. Add all the listed ingredients to a blender
2. Blend until you have a smooth and creamy texture
3. Serve chilled and enjoy!

Per Serving
Calories: 430| Fat: 30g | Protein: 7g | Carbohydrates: 10g | Fiber: 10g | Sugar: 30g| Sodium: 402mg

Goji Berry Wake Up Yoghurt

Prep time: 10 minutes | Cook time: 0 minutes | Serves 2

2 tablespoons Goji berries 2 cups raspberries 2 cups blueberries 3 tablespoons flaxseed powder (or	ground flaxseed) 6 ounces plain or vanilla yogurt (low fat) 2 cups purified water or juice

1. Set your Vitamix to variable 1.
2. Turn your Vitamix on, and gradually move up to variable 10, once at variable 10 switch to High.
3. Blend this energizing smoothie on high for 45 seconds or until desired consistency is reached.

Per Serving
Calories: 427| Fat: 8g | Protein: 11g | Carbohydrates: 79g | Fiber: 17g | Sugar: 106g| Sodium: 636mg

Berry and Avocado Anti-Wrinkle Smoothie

Prep time: 10 minutes | Cook time: 0 minutes | Serves 2

2 cups blueberries 2 medium avocados (peeled and pitted) 2 tablespoons flaxseed (ground if possible)	2 ½ cups coconut water 2 tablespoons honey (or your choice of sweetener)

1. Set your Vitamix to variable 1.
2. Turn your Vitamix on, and gradually move up to variable 10, once at variable 10 switch to High.
3. Enjoy this delicious smoothie after blending on high for about 40 seconds, or until desired consistency is reached.

Per Serving
Calories: 547| Fat: 33g | Protein: 8g | Carbohydrates: 64g | Fiber: 19g | Sugar: 79g| Sodium: 547mg

Limey Fruit with Spinach and Cilantro

Prep time: 10 minutes | Cook time: 0 minutes | Serves 1

1 tablespoon agave nectar 1 bunch kale, spinach, Swiss chard or combination 1 bunch cilantro 2 cucumbers,	chopped and peeled 1 lime, peeled 1 lemon, outer yellow peeled 1 orange, peeled ½ cup ice

1. Add all the listed ingredients to a blender
2. Blend until you have a smooth and creamy texture
3. Serve chilled and enjoy!

Per Serving
Calories: 3,180| Fat: 15g | Protein: 5g | Carbohydrates: 8g | Fiber: 7g | Sugar: 15g| Sodium: 45mg

Nut and Berry Wrinkle Fighter

Prep time: 10 minutes | Cook time: 0 minutes | Serves 1

2 brazil nuts 1 tablespoon flaxseeds 1 orange, peeled and cut in half 2 cups wild	blueberries, frozen 2 cups kale, roughly chopped 1 ½ cups cold coconut water

1. Add all the listed ingredients to a blender
2. Blend until you have a smooth and creamy texture
3. Serve chilled and enjoy!

Per Serving
Calories: 180| Fat: 15g | Protein: 5g | Carbohydrates: 8g | Fiber: 10g | Sugar: 30g| Sodium: 402mg

Lemony Kale and Carrot Glass

Prep time: 10 minutes | Cook time: 0 minutes | Serves 1

1 cup of coconut water
Lemon juice, 1 lemon
1 green apple, core
removed and chopped
1 carrot, chopped
1 cup kale

1. Add all the listed ingredients to a blender
2. Blend until you have a smooth and creamy texture
3. Serve chilled and enjoy!

Per Serving
Calories: 116| Fat: 5g | Protein: 6g | Carbohydrates: 14g | Fiber: 9g | Sugar: 30g| Sodium: 302mg

Mango and Pineapple with Chia Glass

Prep time: 5 minutes | Cook time: 0 minutes | Serves 1

1 cup coconut water
1 tablespoon chia seeds
1 cup pineapple, sliced
½ cup mango, sliced

1. Add all the listed ingredients to a blender
2. Blend until you have a smooth and creamy texture
3. Serve chilled and enjoy!

Per Serving
Calories: 90| Fat: 5g | Protein: 4g | Carbohydrates: 11g | Fiber: 6g | Sugar: 53g| Sodium: 255mg

Almond with Anti-Aging Cacao

Prep time: 5 minutes | Cook time: 0 minutes | Serves 1

1 cup unsweetened almond milk
1 tablespoon cacao
powder
6 strawberries
1 banana

1. Add all the listed ingredients to a blender
2. Blend until you have a smooth and creamy texture
3. Serve chilled and enjoy!

Per Serving
Calories: 220| Fat: 9g | Protein: 6g | Carbohydrates: 20g | Fiber: 5g | Sugar: 30g| Sodium: 112mg

Flaxseed and Orange Anti-Ultra Violet

Prep time: 5 minutes | Cook time: 0 minutes | Serves 2

2 ½ cups coconut water
1 ½ oranges (sliced, peeled and seeds removed)
2 kiwis (peeled and
sliced)
2 tablespoons flaxseeds (preferably ground or in powder form)

1. Set your Vitamix to variable 1.
2. Turn your Vitamix on, and gradually move up to variable 10, once at variable 10 switch to High.
3. Enjoy this delicious smoothie after blending on high for 45 seconds or until desired consistency is reached.

Per Serving
Calories: 205| Fat: 3g | Protein: 6g | Carbohydrates: 41g | Fiber: 11g | Sugar: 16g| Sodium: 319mg

Milky Sunflower and Fruit Green

Prep time: 10 minutes | Cook time: 0 minutes | Serves 2

1 ½ bananas
1 ½ cups spinach (chopped)
¼ cup avocado (peeled and pit removed)
2 tablespoons sunflower seeds
¼ cup lemon juice (no
seeds)
2 ½ cups soy or almond milk (low fat dairy milk is okay too)
3 tablespoons sweetener (your choice)

1. Set your Vitamix to variable 1.
2. Turn your Vitamix on, and gradually move up to variable 10, once at variable 10 switch to High.
3. Enjoy this delicious smoothie after blending on high for 45 seconds or until desired consistency is reached.

Per Serving
Calories: 835| Fat: 72g | Protein: 10g | Carbohydrates: 44g | Fiber: 13g | Sugar: 38g| Sodium: 71mg

Chapter 7: Detoxification Recipes

Lime and Milky Detox Smoothie

Prep time: 10 minutes | Cook time: 0 minutes | Serves 2

1 frozen sliced very ripe banana, previously peeled & sliced
¼ cup almond milk
1 ¼ cups chopped pineapple
1 peach, peeled and sliced
½ cup Greek yogurt
2 cups fresh spinach
Juice and zest of 1 lime, optional (provides great flavor)

1. Add liquid first, then softer ingredients and harder items like ice or frozen fruit last.
2. Blend on medium and increase to high for 1 minute.
3. Repeat as necessary.

Per Serving
Calories: 170| Fat: 1g | Protein: 5g | Carbohydrates: 37g | Fiber: 2g | Sugar: 33g| Sodium: 97mg

Lemony Green Tea Detox Smoothie

Prep time: 10 minutes | Cook time: 0 minutes | Serves 2

1 navel orange
1 grapefruit
the juice of half a lemon
½ cup of unsweetened green tea, chilled
½ cup of nonfat
Greek yogurt
½ a frozen banana
1 cup of ice
½ tablespoon honey
optional garnishes orange/grapefruit/ lemon zest on top

1. Add liquid first, then softer ingredients and harder items like ice or frozen fruit last.
2. Blend on medium and increase to high for 1 minute.
3. Repeat as necessary.

Per Serving
Calories: 292| Fat: 9g | Protein: 2g | Carbohydrates: 50g | Fiber: 6g | Sugar: 34g| Sodium: 69mg

Blueberry Fruit Detox Smoothie

Prep time: 5 minutes | Cook time: 0 minutes | Serves 1

½ cup frozen blueberries
¼ cup unsweetened
cranberry juice
2 bananas

1. Add liquid first, then softer ingredients and harder items like ice or frozen fruit last.
2. Blend on medium and increase to high for 1 minute.
3. Repeat as necessary.

Per Serving
Calories: 72| Fat: 1g | Protein: 8g | Carbohydrates: 71g | Fiber: 8g | Sugar: 42g| Sodium: 4mg

Turmeric and Cranberry Bliss Detox Smoothie

Prep time: 15 minutes | Cook time: 0 minutes | Serves 2

2 apples, sliced, peel left on
2 pears, sliced, peel left on
1 lemon, peeled, cut in quarters, seeds removed
1 cup fresh cranberries
2 cups of filtered
water
Sweetener of choice
6 Ice cubes
1 tablespoon turmeric
2 teaspoons pumpkin pie spice blend (optional)
OR 2 teaspoons of cinnamon or 1 teaspoon of nutmeg

1. Add liquid first, then softer ingredients and harder items like ice or frozen fruit last.
2. Blend on medium and increase to high for 1 minute.
3. Repeat as necessary.

Per Serving
Calories: 349| Fat: 2g | Protein: 2g | Carbohydrates: 91g | Fiber: 16g | Sugar: 65g| Sodium: 20mg

Ginger Avocado with Cucumber and Lemon

Prep time: 15 minutes | Cook time: 0 minutes | Serves 2

½ avocado
½ cucumber
½ pear
¼ lemon
¼ cup cilantro
¾-inch ginger (sliced)

1 ½ cups kale (tightly packed)
¾ cups coconut water
¼ cup protein powder
2 cups water

1. Set your Vitamix to variable 1.
2. Turn your Vitamix on, and gradually move up to variable 10, once at variable 10 switch to High.
3. Blend this scrumptious smoothie on high for 45 seconds, or until desired consistency is reached.

Per Serving
Calories: 236| Fat: 11g | Protein: 14g | Carbohydrates: 23g | Fiber: 7g | Sugar: 5g| Sodium: 189mg

Pineapple with Kale Detox Smoothie

Prep time: 5 minutes | Cook time: 0 minutes | Serves 2

4 cups kale, chopped
2 cups of coconut water

2 bananas
2 cups pineapple

1. Add all the listed ingredients to a blender
2. Blend until you have a smooth and creamy texture
3. Serve chilled and enjoy!

Per Serving
Calories: 316| Fat: 1g | Protein:5g | Carbohydrates: 78g | Fiber: 9g | Sugar: 57g| Sodium: 268mg

Ginger with Lemony Detox Drink

Prep time: 5 minutes | Cook time: 0 minutes | Serves 1

1 (12-ounce) glass water, at room temperature

Juice of ½ lemon
½ inch knob of ginger root

1. Add liquid first, then softer ingredients and harder items like ice or frozen fruit last.

2. Blend on medium and increase to high for 1 minute. Repeat as necessary.

Per Serving
Calories: 6| Fat: 0g | Protein: 0g | Carbohydrates: 2g | Fiber: 0g | Sugar: 1g| Sodium: 7mg

Minty Lettuce and Berry with Apple

Prep time: 10 minutes | Cook time: 0 minutes | Serves 2

½ cup mixed berries (frozen or fresh)
10 leaves of mint
1 apple (peeled, sliced and seeds removed)

5 romaine lettuce leaves
20 ounces purified water (use juice if desired)

1. Set your Vitamix to variable 1.
2. Turn your Vitamix on, and gradually move up to variable 10, once at variable 10 switch to High.
3. Blend this delicious smoothie on high for 45 seconds, or until desired consistency is reached.

Per Serving
Calories: 93| Fat: 1g | Protein: 2g | Carbohydrates: 22g | Fiber: 7g | Sugar: 5g| Sodium: 18mg

Clementine with Carrot Detox Smoothie

Prep time: 10 minutes | Cook time: 0 minutes | Serves 1

1 carrot, peeled, sliced
1 beet, peeled, sliced
½ cup red grapes
1 clementine, peeled

1 slice of ginger, peeled, about the size of a quarter
½ cup green tea

1. Add liquid first, then softer ingredients and harder items like ice or frozen fruit last.
2. Blend on medium and increase to high for 1 minute.
3. Repeat as necessary.

Per Serving
Calories: 53| Fat: 0g | Protein: 1g | Carbohydrates: 15g | Fiber: 2g | Sugar: 12g| Sodium: 35mg

Moringa with Hazelnut Detox Smoothie

Prep time: 10 minutes | Cook time: 0 minutes | Serves 1

3 tablespoons collard greens
2 ribs celery
3 springs mint
1 apple, chopped

2 tablespoons hazelnuts, raw
½ teaspoon moringa
1 cup of water
1 cup ice

1. Add all the listed ingredients to a blender
2. Blend until you have a smooth and creamy texture
3. Serve chilled and enjoy!

Per Serving
Calories: 351| Fat: 28g | Protein:1g | Carbohydrates: 28g | Fiber: 6g | Sugar: 20g| Sodium: 17mg

Tomato with Zucchini Detox Smoothie

Prep time: 10 minutes | Cook time: 0 minutes | Serves 2

1 zucchini
1 tablespoon sea beans
½ lemon, juiced
1 teaspoon maqui berry powder
8 tablespoons grape

tomatoes
6 tablespoons celery stocks
½ jalapeno pepper, seeded
1 cup of water
1 cup ice

1. Add all the listed ingredients to blender except zucchini
2. Add zucchini and blend the mixture
3. Blend until smooth
4. Serve chilled and enjoy!

Per Serving
Calories: 50| Fat: 0g | Protein:3g | Carbohydrates: 10g | Fiber: 6g | Sugar: 19g| Sodium: 17mg

Turmeric with Carrot Detox Smoothie

Prep time: 10 minutes | Cook time: 0 minutes | Serves 2

10 tablespoons carrot, chopped
1-inch ginger, peeled and chopped
1 teaspoon cinnamon

1 banana, peeled
1-inch turmeric peeled, chopped
1 cup of coconut milk
1 cup ice

1. Add all the listed ingredients to a blender

2. Blend until smooth
3. Serve chilled and enjoy!

Per Serving
Calories: 203| Fat: 5g | Protein:7g | Carbohydrates: 36g | Fiber: 9g | Sugar: 21g| Sodium: 263mg

Lemon and Pear Detox Smoothie

Prep time: 10 minutes | Cook time: 0 minutes | Serves 2

3 tablespoons red kale
8 tablespoons jicama, peeled and chopped
1 lemon, juiced
1 pear, chopped

1 teaspoon reishi mushroom
1 tablespoon flaxseed
1 cup of water
1 cup ice

1. Add all the listed ingredients to a blender
2. Blend until smooth
3. Serve chilled and enjoy!

Per Serving
Calories: 102| Fat: 0g | Protein:2g | Carbohydrates: 24g | Fiber: 11g | Sugar: 28g| Sodium: 264mg

Lemony Chia and Ginger Beet

Prep time: 10 minutes | Cook time: 0 minutes | Serves 2

1 medium sized beet (cleaned and sliced)
2 apples (peeled, sliced and seeds and core removed)
⅓ cup parsley
2 tablespoons chia seeds

¾ inches of ginger
1 ½ lemons (peeled, sliced and seeds removed)
2 cups kale leaves (chopped)
16 ounces purified water

1. Set your Vitamix to variable 1.
2. Turn your Vitamix on, and gradually move up to variable 10, once at variable 10 switch to High.
3. Blend all ingredients on high for 1 minute, or until desired consistency is reached.

Per Serving
Calories: 326| Fat: 10g | Protein: 10g | Carbohydrates: 52g | Fiber: 17g | Sugar: 5g| Sodium: 71mg

Swiss Chard Pineapple Detox Smoothie

Prep time: 10 minutes | Cook time: 0 minutes | Serves 2

3 tablespoons Swiss chard	pineapple, peeled and chopped
2 tablespoons coconut flakes	½ avocado pitted
1 tablespoon chia seeds	1 orange, peeled
8 tablespoons	1 cup of water
	1 cup ice

1. Add all the listed ingredients to a blender
2. Blend until smooth
3. Serve chilled and enjoy!

Per Serving
Calories: 212| Fat: 0g | Protein:3g | Carbohydrates: 2g | Fiber: 4g | Sugar: 6g| Sodium: 29mg

Spinach and Avocado Detox Smoothie

Prep time: 5 minutes | Cook time: 0 minutes | Serves 3

4 cups spinach, chopped	3 cups apple juice
1 avocado, chopped	2 apples, unpeeled, cored and chopped

1. Add all the listed ingredients to a blender
2. Blend until you have a smooth and creamy texture
3. Serve chilled and enjoy!

Per Serving
Calories: 336| Fat: 14g | Protein:3g | Carbohydrates: 56g | Fiber: 9g | Sugar: 37g| Sodium: 47mg

Lemony Chamomile and Ginger Detox Smoothie

Prep time: 10 minutes | Cook time: 0 minutes | Serves 2

3 tablespoons collard greens	1 cantaloupe, sliced and chopped
1 tablespoon chamomile flowers, dried	½ inch ginger, peeled
1 pear, chopped	½ lemon, juiced
	1 cup ice
	1 cup of water

1. Add all the listed ingredients to a blender
2. Blend until smooth
3. Serve chilled and enjoy!

Per Serving
Calories: 57| Fat: 0g | Protein:0g | Carbohydrates: 15g | Fiber: 3g | Sugar: 10g| Sodium: 5mg

Kiwi with Wheatgrass Detox Smoothie

Prep time: 10 minutes | Cook time: 0 minutes | Serves 2

3 tablespoons Swiss chard	1 teaspoon wheatgrass powder
1 banana, peeled	2 kiwis, peeled
3 tablespoons almonds	1 cup ice
	1 cup of water

1. Add all the listed ingredients to blender except kiwis
2. Blend until smooth
3. Add kiwis and blend again
4. Serve chilled and enjoy!

Per Serving
Calories: 154| Fat: 6g | Protein:4g | Carbohydrates: 24g | Fiber: 3g | Sugar: 10g| Sodium: 5mg

Milky Almond Detox Berry

Prep time: 10 minutes | Cook time: 0 minutes | Serves 2

⅔ cups frozen cherries (pitted)	honey
1 cup frozen raspberries	1 ½ tablespoons ginger (finely grated)
1 cup rice milk or almond milk	2 tablespoons flaxseeds
2 ½ tablespoons	1 tablespoons lemon juice

1. Set your Vitamix to variable 1.
2. Turn your Vitamix on, and gradually move up to variable 10, once at variable 10 switch to High.
3. Blend this tasty smoothie for 45 seconds on high, or until desired consistency is reached.

Per Serving
Calories: 321| Fat: 2.4g | Protein: 3g | Carbohydrates: 76g | Fiber: 8g | Sugar: 2g| Sodium: 49mg

Ginger Lemonade Detox Smoothie

Prep time: 10 minutes | Cook time: 0 minutes | Serves 2

3 tablespoons collard green
½ teaspoon charcoal activated
1 apple, chopped

1 lemon, peeled
½ inch ginger
1 cucumber, chopped
1 cup ice
1 cup of water

1. Add all the listed ingredients to blender except kiwis
2. Blend until smooth
3. Add kiwis and blend again
4. Serve chilled and enjoy!

Per Serving
Calories: 88| Fat: 1g | Protein: 2g |
Carbohydrates: 23g | Fiber: 3g | Sugar: 11g|
Sodium: 6mg

Apple Cider Detox Remedy Drink

Prep time: 5 minutes | Cook time: 0 minutes | Serves 1

25 ounces cold water
2 tablespoon apple cider vinegar
Optional:
Cinnamon

1 full lemon
Ice

Stevia

1. Add liquid first, then softer ingredients and harder items like ice or frozen fruit last.
2. Blend on medium and increase to high for 1 minute.
3. Repeat as necessary.

Per Serving
Calories: 17| Fat: 0g | Protein: 0g |
Carbohydrates: 0g | Fiber: 4g | Sugar: 11g|
Sodium: 16mg

Pineapple Matcha with Mango Smoothie

Prep time: 10 minutes | Cook time: 0 minutes | Serves 2

1½ teaspoon matcha green tea
1 scoop protein powder
some honey
1 cup frozen mango

chunks
1 tablespoon pineapple juice
1 pineapple
½ cup of water

1. Add liquid first, then softer ingredients and harder items like ice or frozen fruit last.
2. Blend on medium and increase to high for 1 minute.
3. Repeat as necessary.

Per Serving
Calories: 330| Fat: 2g | Protein: 10g |
Carbohydrates: 75g | Fiber: 8g | Sugar: 54g|
Sodium: 38mg

Cinnamon with Kale Power Detox Smoothie

Prep time: 10 minutes | Cook time: 0 minutes | Serves 1

1 cup of apples, cored and chopped into cubes with peel on (preferably fresh and organic)
1 cup of pears, cored and chopped into cubes with peel on (preferably fresh and organic)
2 to 3 tablespoon of freshly squeezed lime juice (preferably fresh and organic)
1 cup of kale

(preferably fresh and organic)
¼ cup of flat leaf parsley (preferably fresh and organic)
½ cup of chopped celery stalk (preferably fresh and organic)
1 tablespoon flax seeds (ground)
¼ tablespoon cinnamon powder
1 cup of purified water (chilled)

1. Wilt the kale using steam or in a pan. Set aside for it to cool.
2. In your Vitamix Blender, combine the wilted kale, celery stalk, parsley, and purified water. Blend until the greens are properly broken down.
3. Add in the cubed apples and pears, and lime juice. Blend until the mixture is smooth in consistency.
4. Finally, add in the flax seeds and cinnamon powder. Pulse two or three more times until added ingredients are properly incorporated into the mixture. Do not over blend to avoid losing the nutrients.
5. Pour into a glass. Serve and drink up right away. Enjoy!

Per Serving
Calories: 336| Fat: 4g | Protein: 5g |
Carbohydrates: 75g | Fiber: 10g | Sugar: 54g| Sodium: 75mg

Berry Spirulina with Avocado

Prep time: 10 minutes | Cook time: 0 minutes | Serves 2

1 banana	1 tablespoon spirulina
½ avocado	powder
1 cup almond milk or	½ cup protein powder
soymilk	2 cups water
1 cup blueberries	

1. Set your Vitamix to variable 1.
2. Turn your Vitamix on, and gradually move up to variable 10, once at variable 10 switch to High.
3. Blend this delicious smoothie on high for 45 seconds, or until desired consistency is reached.

Per Serving
Calories: 542| Fat: 40g | Protein: 17g | Carbohydrates: 39g | Fiber: 9g | Sugar: 36g| Sodium: 126mg

Celery Mango Super Cleanse

Prep time: 10 minutes | Cook time: 0 minutes | Serves 2

1 cup kale (or romaine	¼ cup parsley
lettuce)	(chopped)
1 cup orange juice	1 stalk celery
½ cup mango (sliced)	(chopped)

1. Set your Vitamix to variable 1.
2. Turn your Vitamix on, and gradually move up to variable 10, once at variable 10 switch to High.
3. Blend all ingredients on high for 30 to 45 seconds, or until desired consistency is reached.

Per Serving
Calories: 149| Fat: 1g | Protein: 3g | Carbohydrates: 34g | Fiber: 3g | Sugar: 16g| Sodium: 29mg

Orange and Parsley with Mango Detox

Prep time: 10 minutes | Cook time: 0 minutes | Serves 2

1 ½ cups orange juice	1 ½ cups cubed
¼ cup chopped	mango
parsley	1 ½ cups chopped
1 ½ chopped celery	kale leaves
stems	

1. Set your Vitamix to variable 1.
2. Turn your Vitamix on, and gradually move up to variable 10, once at variable 10 switch to High.
3. Blend all ingredients for 45 seconds, or until desired consistency is reached.

Per Serving
Calories: 151| Fat: 1g | Protein: 4g | Carbohydrates: 35g | Fiber: 3g | Sugar: 34g| Sodium: 43mg

Goji Berry with Banana and Strawberry

Prep time: 10 minutes | Cook time: 0 minutes | Serves 2

2 bananas	2 ½ cups coconut
½ cup strawberries	water
(frozen or fresh)	4 ice cubes
½ cup Goji berries	

1. Set your Vitamix to variable 1.
2. Turn your Vitamix on, and gradually move up to variable 10, once at variable 10 switch to High.
3. Blend all ingredients on high for about 45 seconds or until desired consistency is reached.

Per Serving
Calories: 214| Fat: 2g | Protein: 5g | Carbohydrates: 51g | Fiber: 8g | Sugar: 10g| Sodium: 361mg

Banana Berry with Blue Ginger

Prep time: 10 minutes | Cook time: 0 minutes | Serves 2

½ cup blueberries	½ cup ginger juice
2 bananas (fresh or	2 ½ cups soy milk
frozen	(almond milk or low
4 ice cubes	calorie milk is fine)

1. Set your Vitamix to variable 1.
2. Turn your Vitamix on, and gradually move up to variable 10, once at variable 10 switch to High.
3. Blend all ingredients on high for 45 seconds, or until desired consistency is reached.

Per Serving
Calories: 366| Fat: 7g | Protein: 13g | Carbohydrates: 67g | Fiber: 9g | Sugar: 29g| Sodium: 179mg

Carrot Spring Cleaning Detox

Prep time: 10 minutes | Cook time: 0 minutes | Serves 2

1 teaspoon of whole flax seeds.
1 red apple, peeled and sliced.
8 snack-sized peeled carrots (or 2 normal carrots, peeled and

chopped).
¼ inch nub of fresh ginger root, skin removed. (should be moist)
1 cup of lukewarm water.

1. Add liquid first, then softer ingredients and harder items like ice or frozen fruit last.
2. Blend on medium and increase to high for 1 minute.
3. Repeat as necessary.

Per Serving
Calories: 120| Fat: 1g | Protein: 2g | Carbohydrates: 28g | Fiber: 8g | Sugar: 16g| Sodium: 110mg

Cilantro Algae with Kale

Prep time: 15 minutes | Cook time: 0 minutes | Serves 2

4 kale leaves (chopped)
½ cup spinach (chopped)
2 ½ cups coconut water
½ cup parsley leaves (no stems)

½ cup cilantro
2 apples (green preferably)
½ ginger root (grated)
2 tablespoons blue-green algae powder

1. Set your Vitamix to variable 1.
2. Turn your Vitamix on, and gradually move up to variable 10, once at variable 10 switch to High.
3. Blend the smoothie on high for about 55 seconds, or until desired consistency is reached.

Per Serving
Calories: 256| Fat: 1g | Protein: 13g | Carbohydrates: 51g | Fiber: 11g | Sugar: 27g| Sodium: 391mg

Ginger with Lemon Cilantro Detox

Prep time: 10 minutes | Cook time: 0 minutes | Serves 2

½ avocado (sliced)
¼ lemon (peeled and de-seeded)
½ pear
¼ cucumber (peeled and sliced)
1 cup kale (or romaine

lettuce)
½ ounce sliced ginger
3 ounces protein powder (hemp or pea)
3 tablespoons cilantro (chopped)

1. Set your Vitamix to variable 1.
2. Turn your Vitamix on, and gradually move up to variable 10, once at variable 10 switch to High.
3. Blend all ingredients on high for 30 to 45 seconds, or until desired consistency is reached.

Per Serving
Calories: 334| Fat: 13g | Protein: 33g | Carbohydrates: 25g | Fiber: 6g | Sugar: 3g| Sodium: 98mg

Peach and Mint Tea Smoothie

Prep time: 10 minutes | Cook time: 0 minutes | Serves 1

1 cup of green tea (freshly brewed then chilled)
½ cup of peaches, cut into cubes (preferably fresh and organic)
½ cup of mangoes, cut into cubes

(preferably fresh and organic)
2 tablespoon of freshly squeezed lime juice
A handful of mint leaves

1. Combine all the ingredients in your Vitamix Blender. Blend until the mixture is smooth in consistency. If you want a refreshingly cool drink, chill the ingredients first before blending them together. Do not over blend to avoid losing the nutrients.
2. Pour into a glass. Serve and drink up right away. Enjoy!

Per Serving
Calories: 156| Fat: 0g | Protein: 1g | Carbohydrates: 42g | Fiber: 3g | Sugar: 36g| Sodium: 16mg

Cucumber Celery Cranberry

Prep time: 10 minutes | Cook time: 0 minutes | Serves 2

2 cups purified water or cranberry juice
¾ cups cranberries
1 cucumber (peeled)
1 celery stalk (sliced)
1 ½ apples (peeled, cored and seeds removed)
1 ½ pears (cored)
½ cup spinach

1. Set your Vitamix to variable 1.
2. Turn your Vitamix on, and gradually move up to variable 10, once at variable 10 switch to High.
3. Blend all ingredients on high for about one minute or until desired consistency is reached.

Per Serving
Calories: 247| Fat: 0g | Protein: 3g | Carbohydrates: 64g | Fiber: 15g | Sugar: 57g| Sodium: 21mg

Maple Berry with Avocado Sunrise Smoothie

Prep time: 10 minutes | Cook time: 0 minutes | Serves 1 to 2

½ avocado
½ cup fresh squeezed orange juice
1 cup fresh squeezed grapefruit juice
1 cup DOLE frozen strawberries
¾ cup DOLE banana (use frozen banana slices for thicker smoothie)
¼ cup ice
1 teaspoon maple syrup (optional)

1. Add liquid first, then softer ingredients and harder items like ice or frozen fruit last.
2. Blend on medium and increase to high for 1 minute.
3. Repeat as necessary.

Per Serving
Calories: 333| Fat: 10g | Protein: 4g | Carbohydrates: 63g | Fiber: 9g | Sugar: 47g| Sodium: 19mg

Lemon and Honey Tangy Blueberry

Prep time: 5 minutes | Cook time: 0 minutes | Serves 2

½ cup blueberries
2 lemons (peeled, sliced and seeds removed)
2 tablespoons
sweetener (honey, or your choice)
2 ½ cups purified water

1. Set your Vitamix to variable 1.
2. Turn your Vitamix on, and gradually move up to variable 10, once at variable 10 switch to High.
3. Blend this deliciously tangy smoothie on high for about 45 seconds, or until desired consistency is reached.

Per Serving
Calories: 38| Fat: 0g | Protein: 1g | Carbohydrates: 13g | Fiber: 4g | Sugar: 21g| Sodium: 1mg

Lettuce and Mango with Lemon

Prep time: 10 minutes | Cook time: 0 minutes | Serves 2

1 ½ lemons (peeled, sliced and seeds removed)
2 apples (green preferably)
1 cucumber (peeled)
5 leaves of red lettuce
½ cup mango cubes (frozen or fresh)
2 teaspoons barley grass powder
16 ounces purified water

1. Set your Vitamix to variable 1.
2. Turn your Vitamix on, and gradually move up to variable 10, once at variable 10 switch to High.
3. Blend all ingredients on high for about 45 seconds, or until desired consistency is reached.

Per Serving
Calories: 188| Fat: 7g | Protein: 3g | Carbohydrates: 48g | Fiber: 8g | Sugar: 27g| Sodium: 18mg

Fruity Detox Special

Prep time: 10 minutes | Cook time: 0 minutes | Serves 2

1 ½ tablespoons lemon zest
2 ½ cups strawberries (fresh or frozen)
3 ½ cups non-dairy
milk (your choice)
1 orange (peeled)
1 ½ bananas
2 cups spinach

1. Set your Vitamix to variable 1.
2. Turn your Vitamix on, and gradually move up to variable 10, once at variable 10 switch to High.
3. Blend this sweet for 45 seconds, or until desired consistency is reached.

Per Serving
Calories: 364| Fat: 7g | Protein: 16g | Carbohydrates: 64g | Fiber: 11g | Sugar: 9g| Sodium: 245mg

Creamy Berry and Coconut Shake

Prep time: 10 minutes | Cook time: 0 minutes | Serves 1

½ cup organic fresh blueberries
½ cup organic fresh strawberries
½ cup organic fresh raspberries
½ cup coconut cream
½ cup coconut water

1. In your Vitamix Blender, mix in the blueberries, strawberries, raspberries, and coconut water. Blend well.
2. Add in the coconut cream. Blend until smooth. Do not over blend to avoid losing the nutrients.
3. Pour into a glass. Serve and drink up right away. Enjoy!

Per Serving
Calories: 671| Fat: 8g | Protein: 43g | Carbohydrates: 76g | Fiber: 12g | Sugar: 59g| Sodium: 139mg

Limey Cucumber with Cilantro and Kale

Prep time: 10 minutes | Cook time: 0 minutes | Serves 2

½ cucumber (sliced)
1 cup kale (or romaine lettuce or spinach)
1 ½ cups spring water
⅓ cup cilantro (chopped)
½ lemon (peeled and de-seeded)
1 wedge lime (peeled and de-seeded)
½ cup cilantro

1. Set your Vitamix to variable 1.
2. Turn your Vitamix on, and gradually move up to variable 10, once at variable 10 switch to High.
3. Blend all ingredients on high for 30 -45 seconds, or until desired consistency is reached.

Per Serving
Calories: 39| Fat: 0g | Protein: 2g | Carbohydrates: 10g | Fiber: 2g | Sugar: 2g| Sodium: 20mg

Berry Flaxseed with Dates

Prep time: 10 minutes | Cook time: 0 minutes | Serves 2

1½ cups blueberries
1 ½ cups coconut milk
¾ cups blackberries
¾ cups raspberries
¼ cup Goji berries (These should soak
for 10-15 minutes before blending)
2 tablespoons flaxseed (ground)
5 dates (pitted)
2 cups purified water

1. Set your Vitamix to variable 1.
2. Turn your Vitamix on, and gradually move up to variable 10, once at variable 10 switch to High.
3. Blend the smoothie on high for about 50 seconds, or until desired consistency is reached, and start feeling good.

Per Serving
Calories: 659| Fat: 47g | Protein: 10g | Carbohydrates: 64g | Fiber: 17g | Sugar: 2g| Sodium: 61mg

Milky Pear and Chia with Protein

Prep time: 10 minutes | Cook time: 0 minutes | Serves 2

2 cups almond milk or soymilk
½ avocado
1 pear (sliced)
1 ½ cups spinach (tightly packed)

1/2 cup coconut water
1 tablespoon chia seeds
½ cup protein powder
2 ½ cups water

1. Set your Vitamix to variable 1.
2. Turn your Vitamix on, and gradually move up to variable 10, once at variable 10 switch to High.
3. Blend this delicious smoothie for 45 seconds on high, or until desired consistency is reached.

Per Serving
Calories: 849| Fat: 73g | Protein: 21g | Carbohydrates: 39g | Fiber: 17g | Sugar: 5g| Sodium: 189mg

Romaine and Avocado with Jicama

Prep time: 10 minutes | Cook time: 0 minutes | Serves 2

1 lime
1 cucumber
1 apple
10 romaine leaves
1 avocado
1 cup jicama (grated

or sliced)
½ cup cilantro
½ cup protein powder
3 pitted dates
2 ½ cups water

1. Set your Vitamix to variable 1.
2. Turn your Vitamix on, and gradually move up to variable 10, once at variable 10 switch to High.
3. Blend this scrumptious smoothie for 45 seconds on high, or until desired consistency is reached.

Per Serving
Calories: 407| Fat: 21g | Protein: 15g | Carbohydrates: 49g | Fiber: 15g | Sugar: 45g| Sodium: 85mg

Minty Apple and Cucumber with Lime

Prep time: 10 minutes | Cook time: 0 minutes | Serves 2

2 apples (peeled, cored and seeds removed)
1 ½ limes (peeled, sliced and seeds removed)
¾ cups parsley (leaves only, no stems)

2 tablespoons coconut oil
3 tablespoons leaves of mint
1 large cucumber (peeled)
1 cup coconut water
2 cups purified water or juice

1. Set your Vitamix to variable 1.
2. Turn your Vitamix on, and gradually move up to variable 10, once at variable 10 switch to High.
3. Blend all ingredients together for 50 seconds, or until desired consistency is reached.

Per Serving
Calories: 420| Fat: 15g | Protein: 3g | Carbohydrates: 77g | Fiber: 8g | Sugar: 34g| Sodium: 161mg

Tomato and Spinach with Spicy Carrot

Prep time: 10 minutes | Cook time: 0 minutes | Serves 2

3 tomatoes
5 carrots
2 bell peppers (preferably red – sliced and seeds removed)

3 garlic cloves
3 celery stalks
1 cup spinach
1 red jalapeno (seeds removed)
½ cup water cress

1. Set your Vitamix to variable 1.
2. Turn your Vitamix on, and gradually move up to variable 10, once at variable 10 switch to High.
3. Blend all ingredients on high for 45 seconds, or until desired consistency is reached.

Per Serving
Calories: 141| Fat: 1g | Protein: 4g | Carbohydrates: 31g | Fiber: 9g | Sugar: 15g| Sodium: 410mg

Chapter 8: Energy Boosting and Protein Refuel Recipes

Banana Medjool Energy Smoothie

Prep time: 10 minutes | Cook time: 0 minutes | Serves 1

2 medium bananas (Peeled)
3 whole Medjool dates (Pits removed)
1 cup unsweetened

almond milk
1 tablespoon hulled hemp seeds
½ cup ice (optional)

1. Add liquid first, then softer ingredients and harder items like ice or frozen fruit last.
2. Blend on medium and increase to high for 1 minute.
3. Repeat as necessary.

Per Serving
Calories: 376| Fat: 8g | Protein: 11g | Carbohydrates: 68g | Fiber: 7g | Sugar: 47g| Sodium: 70mg

Blueberry Almond Butter Smoothies

Prep time: 10 minutes | Cook time: 0 minutes | Serves 2

1 banana, peeled
1 cup frozen blueberries
½ cup almond butter
½ cup plain yogurt

¾ cup almond milk
3 dates, pitted and quartered
1 cup ice, or as needed

1. Add liquid first, then softer ingredients and harder items like ice or frozen fruit last.
2. Blend on medium and increase to high for 1 minute.
3. Repeat as necessary.

Per Serving
Calories: 493| Fat: 9g | Protein: 13g | Carbohydrates: 36g | Fiber: 12g | Sugar: 57g| Sodium: 90mg

Fruity Energy Boost Smoothie

Prep time: 10 minutes | Cook time: 0 minutes | Serves 2

1 cup of pineapple, peeled and chopped
1 medium orange, peeled
1 cup raspberries

1 medium banana, peeled
1 cup almond milk
1 cup crushed ice

1. Add liquid first, then softer ingredients and harder items like ice or frozen fruit last.
2. Blend on medium and increase to high for 1 minute.
3. Repeat as necessary.

Per Serving
Calories: 493| Fat: 7g | Protein: 13g | Carbohydrates: 57g | Fiber: 12g | Sugar: 68g| Sodium: 90mg

Lemony Veggie Smoothie

Prep time: 10 minutes | Cook time: 0 minutes | Serves 2

2 carrots
3 tomatoes
2 apples
1 cucumber
3 slices of pineapple

4 beets
chunk of ginger
lemon
2 bell peppers

1. Add liquid first, then softer ingredients and harder items like ice or frozen fruit last.
2. Blend on medium and increase to high for 1 minute.
3. Repeat as necessary.

Per Serving
Calories: 231| Fat: 5g | Protein: 1g | Carbohydrates: 57g | Fiber: 10g | Sugar: 41g| Sodium: 59mg

Strawberry Watermelon and Honey Smoothie

Prep time: 5 minutes | Cook time: 0 minutes | Serves 1

1 peeled and sliced mango	4 cups chopped watermelon
10 strawberries depending on tartness	1 tablespoon honey (optional)

1. Add liquid first, then softer ingredients and harder items like ice or frozen fruit last.
2. Blend on medium and increase to high for 1 minute.
3. Repeat as necessary.

Per Serving
Calories: 324| Fat: 5g | Protein: 1g | Carbohydrates: 82g | Fiber: 5g | Sugar: 7g| Sodium: 9mg

Creamy Xanthan and Strawberry Smoothie

Prep time: 10 minutes | Cook time: 0 minutes | Serves 2

1¼ cups of coconut milk	cream
4 tablespoons strawberry	14 large ice cubes
½ cup heavy whipping	½ teaspoon xanthan gum
	2 tablespoons MCT oil

1. Add all the listed ingredients to a blender
2. Blend until you have a smooth and creamy texture
3. Serve chilled and enjoy!

Per Serving
Calories: 373| Fat: 45g | Protein: 2g | Carbohydrates: 5g | Fiber: 4g | Sugar: 7g| Sodium: 34mg

Yoghurt with Citrus Smoothie

Prep time: 10 minutes | Cook time: 0 minutes | Serves 2

2 mangoes, peeled, pit removed and chopped	2 cups Greek yogurt, nonfat
2 bananas	2 cups orange juice
	10 ice cubes

1. Add all the listed ingredients to a blender

2. Blend until you have a smooth and creamy texture
3. Serve chilled and enjoy!

Per Serving
Calories: 379| Fat: 7g | Protein: 9g | Carbohydrates: 76g | Fiber: 9g | Sugar: 92g| Sodium: 122mg

Limey Yoghurt and Cinnamon Smoothie

Prep time: 10 minutes | Cook time: 0 minutes | Serves 1

2 mangoes, peeled, pit removed and chopped	2 teaspoons lime juice
½ teaspoon cinnamon, grounded	2 cups plain yogurt, low-fat
	1 tablespoon honey

1. Add all the listed ingredients to a blender
2. Blend until you have a smooth and creamy texture
3. Serve chilled and enjoy!

Per Serving
Calories: 210| Fat: 2g | Protein: 9g | Carbohydrates: 40g | Fiber: 1g | Sugar: 40g| Sodium: 227mg

Milky Chia with Mango Lassi

Prep time: 10 minutes | Cook time: 0 minutes | Serves 1

2 Large fresh ripe organic mangoes	1 teaspoon of chai spice.
1 banana	1 cup of either almond milk, coconut milk, or coconut water.
½ cup of organic hemp hearts (can substitute coconut meat instead)	

1. Add liquid first, then softer ingredients and harder items like ice or frozen fruit last.
2. Blend on medium and increase to high for 1 minute.
3. Repeat as necessary.

Per Serving
Calories: 443| Fat: 17g | Protein: 5g | Carbohydrates: 74g | Fiber: 8g | Sugar: 56g| Sodium: 182mg

Cinnamon Yoghurt Energy Boost Smoothie

Prep time: 10 minutes | Cook time: 0 minutes | Serves 2

2 tablespoon pure cocoa powder	8 oz nonfat vanilla Greek yogurt
2 tablespoon creamy natural peanut butter	½ cup almond milk
1 medium ripe banana	6 ice cubes
	½ tablespoon cinnamon

1. Add liquid first, then softer ingredients and harder items like ice or frozen fruit last.
2. Blend on medium and increase to high for 1 minute.
3. Repeat as necessary.

Per Serving
Calories: 263| Fat: 18g | Protein: 11g | Carbohydrates: 31g | Fiber: 5g | Sugar: 17g| Sodium: 142mg

Almond and Mango with Honey Smoothie

Prep time: 5 minutes | Cook time: 0 minutes | Serves 1

2 mangoes, peeled, pit removed and chopped	4 teaspoons honey
	3 cups almond milk
	16 ice cubes

1. Add all the listed ingredients to a blender
2. Blend until you have a smooth and creamy texture
3. Serve chilled and enjoy!

Per Serving
Calories: 223| Fat: 3g | Protein: 3g | Carbohydrates: 49g | Fiber: 11g | Sugar: 152g| Sodium: 323mg

Ginger and Pineapple Antioxidant Refresher

Prep time: 5 minutes | Cook time: 0 minutes | Serves 1

4 ounces pineapple	½ teaspoon turmeric
1 orange, peeled	½ teaspoon ginger
1 teaspoon pomegranate powder	1 cup ice
1 mini orange, peeled	1 cup of water

1. Add all the listed ingredients to a blender
2. Blend until you have a smooth and creamy texture
3. Serve chilled and enjoy!

Per Serving
Calories: 101| Fat: 1g | Protein: 2g | Carbohydrates: 25g | Fiber: 11g | Sugar: 33g| Sodium: 10mg

Cherry Protein and Coconut Smoothie

Prep time: 10 minutes | Cook time: 0 minutes | Serves 1

½ cup pitted cherries, frozen or fresh	Juice + flesh from 1 young coconut
¼ cup (30 g / 1 ounce / handful) frozen raspberries	2 scoops whey protein
	1 teaspoon chia seed

1. Add liquid first, then softer ingredients and harder items like ice or frozen fruit last.
2. Blend on medium and increase to high for 1 minute.
3. Repeat as necessary.

Per Serving
Calories: 353| Fat: 36g | Protein: 1g | Carbohydrates: 51g | Fiber: 6g | Sugar: 59g| Sodium: 439mg

Kiwi and Fruity Green Tea Smoothie

Prep time: 10 minutes | Cook time: 0 minutes | Serves 4

2 cups (500 ml) mâché salad (also called lamb's lettuce, valerian, corn salad)	1 ½ banana, frozen
	1 cup pineapple (250 ml)
2 kiwis	1 cup green tea, cold (250 ml)

1. Add liquid first, then softer ingredients and harder items like ice or frozen fruit last.
2. Blend on medium and increase to high for 1 minute.
3. Repeat as necessary.

Per Serving
Calories: 82| Fat: 0g | Protein: 1g | Carbohydrates: 21g | Fiber: 2g | Sugar: 15g| Sodium: 6mg

Milky Flaxseed Berry Burst

Prep time: 10 minutes | Cook time: 0 minutes | Serves 2

1 cup almond or soy milk
½ cup blackberries
½ cup blueberries
1 banana (frozen)

1 tablespoon honey
1 ½ tablespoons flaxseed
½ cup ice cubes

1. Set your Vitamix to variable 1.
2. Turn your Vitamix on, and gradually move up to variable 10, once at variable 10 switch to High.
3. Blend this scrumptious smoothie on high for 30 to 45 seconds, or until desired consistency is reached.

Per Serving
Calories: 423| Fat: 26g | Protein: 12g | Carbohydrates: 43g | Fiber: 12g | Sugar: 100g| Sodium: 5mg

Cauliflower with Raspberry and Chia

Prep time: 10 minutes | Cook time: 0 minutes | Serves 2

1 cup frozen raspberries
2 tablespoons chia seeds
1 cup frozen

cauliflower florets
2 scoops protein powder
½ cup coconut milk
½ cup water

1. Put the raspberries, chia seeds, cauliflower, protein powder, coconut milk, and water in a blender. Blend on high speed until smooth.
2. Divide evenly between 2 cups and enjoy!

Per Serving
Calories: 302| Fat: 19g | Protein: 18g | Carbohydrates: 19g | Fiber: 12g | Sugar: 4g| Sodium: 49mg

Milky Peanut Butter and Oatmeal Smoothie

Prep time: 10 minutes | Cook time: 0 minutes | Serves 2

1 banana
1 cup plain yogurt
2 tablespoon peanut butter

½ cup milk
¼ cup quick-cooking oats and a squirt of honey to taste.

1. Add liquid first, then softer ingredients and harder items like ice or frozen fruit last.
2. Blend on medium and increase to high for 1 minute.
3. Repeat as necessary.

Per Serving
Calories: 340| Fat: 9g | Protein: 8g | Carbohydrates: 61g | Fiber: 2g | Sugar: 53g| Sodium: 326mg

Cucumber with Spinach and Orange Smoothie

Prep time: 10 minutes | Cook time: 0 minutes | Serves 2

3 tablespoons baby spinach
1 apple, chopped
1 lime, peeled
1 cucumber, chopped

1 orange, peeled
1 tablespoon flaxseed
1 cup of water
1 cup ice

1. Add all the listed ingredients to a blender
2. Blend until smooth
3. Serve chilled and enjoy!

Per Serving
Calories: 112| Fat: 2g | Protein: 2g | Carbohydrates: 27g | Fiber: 5g | Sugar: 11g| Sodium: 7mg

Lemony Cucumber Green Machine

Prep time: 10 minutes | Cook time: 0 minutes | Serves 2

1 cup of kale or spinach (chopped)
1 stalk of celery (chopped)
1 apple (sliced)

1 tablespoon lemon juice
⅓ cucumber (sliced)
1 cup ice cubes
¼ cup spring water

1. Set your Vitamix to variable 1.
2. Turn your Vitamix on, and gradually move up to variable 10, once at variable 10 switch to High.
3. Blend all ingredients on high for 30 to 45 seconds, or until desired consistency is reached.

Per Serving
Calories: 62| Fat: 0g | Protein: 1g | Carbohydrates: 15g | Fiber: 3g | Sugar: 16g| Sodium: 26mg

Milk with Ginger Berry Flax Smoothie

Prep time: 10 minutes | Cook time: 0 minutes | Serves 4

3 cups dairy-free milk
2 cups spinach
2 tablespoons flaxseeds, ground

1 cup berries, fresh or frozen
2 teaspoons ginger root, peeled

1. Add all the listed ingredients to a blender
2. Blend until you have a smooth and creamy texture
3. Serve chilled and enjoy!

Per Serving
Calories: 212| Fat: 11g | Protein: 7g | Carbohydrates: 32g | Fiber: 3g | Sugar: 18g| Sodium: 220mg

Apple and Kiwi Green Goblin

Prep time: 10 minutes | Cook time: 0 minutes | Serves 2

1 cup kale or spinach (chopped)
1 apple (peeled, sliced, deseeded)
1/2 cup seedless grapes (green)

1 kiwi (sliced and peeled)
1 cup honeydew melon (shopped and peeled)

1. Set your Vitamix to variable 1.
2. Turn your Vitamix on, and gradually move up to variable 10, once at variable 10 switch to High.
3. Blend all ingredients on high for 30 to 45 seconds, or until desired consistency is reached.

Per Serving
Calories: 133| Fat: 1g | Protein: 2g | Carbohydrates: 33g | Fiber: 5g | Sugar: 43g| Sodium: 32mg

Minty Yoghurt with Chocolate Chip

Prep time: 10 minutes | Cook time: 0 minutes | Serves 2

2 tablespoons raw cacao powder
2 tablespoons chopped fresh mint leaves
2 bananas, halved

and frozen
2 tablespoons chia seeds
1 cup full-fat plain Greek yogurt
1½ cups water

1. Put the cacao powder, mint, bananas, chia seeds, yogurt, and water in a blender.
2. Blend on high speed until smooth.
3. Divide evenly between 2 cups and enjoy!

Per Serving
Calories: 310| Fat: 13g | Protein: 15g | Carbohydrates: 37g | Fiber: 12g | Sugar: 15g| Sodium: 53mg

Kefir and Beet with Blueberry-Almond

Prep time: 10 minutes | Cook time: 0 minutes | Serves 2

1 cup frozen blueberries
1 cup chopped beet greens
¼ cup almonds

2 scoops protein powder
1 cup plain kefir
½ cup water

1. Put the blueberries, beet greens, almonds, protein powder, kefir, and water in a blender.
2. Blend on high speed until smooth.
3. Divide evenly between 2 cups and enjoy!

Per Serving
Calories: 282| Fat: 15g | Protein: 21g | Carbohydrates: 20g | Fiber: 5g | Sugar: 14g| Sodium: 126mg

Almond-Banana-Oat Recovery

Prep time: 10 minutes | Cook time: 0 minutes | Serves 2

2 bananas, halved and frozen
2 tablespoons peanut butter
½ cup rolled oats

2 scoops protein powder
1½ cups unsweetened almond milk

1. Put the bananas, peanut butter, oats, protein powder, and almond milk in a blender.
2. Blend on high speed until smooth.
3. Divide evenly between 2 cups and enjoy!

Per Serving
Calories: 437| Fat: 14g | Protein: 25g | Carbohydrates: 57g | Fiber: 9g | Sugar: 16g| Sodium: 147mg

Walnut and Peach with Cottage Cheese

Prep time: 10 minutes | Cook time: 0 minutes | Serves 2

1 cup frozen sliced peaches
½ cup frozen strawberries
1 cup frozen cauliflower florets
¼ cup chopped walnuts
1 cup full-fat cottage cheese
1 cup water

1. Put the peaches, strawberries, cauliflower, walnuts, cottage cheese, and water in a blender.
2. Blend on high speed until smooth.
3. Divide evenly between 2 cups and enjoy!

Per Serving
Calories: 253| Fat: 14g | Protein: 16g | Carbohydrates: 18g | Fiber: 4g | Sugar: 13g| Sodium: 398mg

Almond with Kale and Banana Power Protein

Prep time: 10 minutes | Cook time: 0 minutes | Serves 2

1 cup chopped kale
1 medium green apple, chopped
1 banana, halved and frozen
2 scoops protein powder
1½ cups unsweetened almond milk

1. Put the kale, apple, banana, protein powder, and almond milk in a blender. Blend on high speed until smooth.
2. Divide evenly between 2 cups and enjoy!

Per Serving
Calories: 203| Fat: 4g | Protein: 15g | Carbohydrates: 30g | Fiber: 5g | Sugar: 16g| Sodium: 158mg

Pomegranate and Berry Energizing Electrolytes

Prep time: 10 minutes | Cook time: 0 minutes | Serves 2

2 cups cubed watermelon, frozen
½ cup pomegranate seeds
½ cup frozen strawberries
2 scoops protein powder
¾ cup coconut water
Pinch Himalayan sea salt

1. Put the watermelon, pomegranate seeds, strawberries, protein powder, coconut water, and salt in a blender.
2. Blend on high speed until smooth.
3. Divide evenly between 2 cups and enjoy!

Per Serving
Calories: 172| Fat: 2g | Protein: 15g | Carbohydrates: 26g | Fiber: 4g | Sugar: 19g| Sodium: 120mg

Banana and Pumpkin Power Smoothie

Prep time: 10 minutes | Cook time: 0 minutes | Serves 2

2 cups pumpkin puree
2 pumpkin pie spice, dashes
1 banana, frozen
2 dashes pie spice, dashes
2 handfuls ice cubes

1. Add all the listed ingredients to a blender
2. Blend until you have a smooth and creamy texture
3. Serve chilled and enjoy!

Per Serving
Calories: 177| Fat: 4g | Protein: 4g | Carbohydrates: 35g | Fiber: 8g | Sugar: 1g| Sodium: 302mg

Berry Yoghurt with Energy Superfood

Prep time: 10 minutes | Cook time: 0 minutes | Serves 2

1 cup frozen pitted cherries
1½ cups frozen mixed berries
1 avocado, peeled and pitted
2 tablespoons chia seeds
2 cups full-fat plain yogurt
½ cup water

1. Put the cherries, berries, avocado, chia seeds, yogurt, and water in a blender. Blend on high speed until smooth.
2. Divide evenly between 2 cups and enjoy!

Per Serving
Calories: 427| Fat: 25g | Protein: 14g | Carbohydrates: 43g | Fiber: 15g | Sugar: 24g| Sodium: 123mg

Spinach Berry with Coconut-Fig

Prep time: 10 minutes | Cook time: 0 minutes | Serves 2

1 cup frozen blackberries	2 scoops protein powder
6 ripe figs, chopped	1 cup coconut milk
1 cup fresh spinach	½ cup water

1. Put the blackberries, figs, spinach, protein powder, coconut milk, and water in a blender.
2. Blend on high speed until smooth.
3. Divide evenly between 2 cups and enjoy!

Per Serving
Calories: 317| Fat: 14g | Protein: 16g | Carbohydrates: 38g | Fiber: 8g | Sugar: 28g| Sodium: 69mg

Kefir Collagen with Cranberry-Orange

Prep time: 10 minutes | Cook time: 0 minutes | Serves 2

1 medium orange, peeled	carrots
½ cup frozen cranberries	1 cup plain kefir
½ cup chopped	3 tablespoons collagen powder
	1½ cups water

1. Put the orange, cranberries, carrots, kefir, collagen powder, and water in a blender.
2. Blend on high speed until smooth.
3. Divide evenly between 2 cups and enjoy!

Per Serving
Calories: 183| Fat: 4g | Protein: 18g | Carbohydrates: 20g | Fiber: 3g | Sugar: 14g| Sodium: 163mg

Kale and Fruity Yoghurt Refresher

Prep time: 10 minutes | Cook time: 0 minutes | Serves 2

1 cup frozen strawberries	1 cup full-fat plain Greek yogurt
1 banana, halved and frozen	1 cup bone broth
1 cup chopped kale	½ cup water

1. Put the strawberries, banana, kale, yogurt, bone broth, and water in a blender.
2. Blend on high speed until smooth.

3. Divide evenly between 2 cups and enjoy!

Per Serving
Calories: 220| Fat: 7g | Protein: 17g | Carbohydrates: 22g | Fiber: 3g | Sugar: 11g| Sodium: 228mg

Limey Banana with Coconut and Cashew

Prep time: 10 minutes | Cook time: 0 minutes | Serves 2

2 bananas, halved and frozen	2 scoops protein powder
1 lime, peeled	½ cup coconut milk
⅓ cup raw cashews	1 cup water

1. Put the bananas, lime, cashews, protein powder, coconut milk, and water in a blender.
2. Blend on high speed until smooth.
3. Divide evenly between 2 cups and enjoy!

Per Serving
Calories: 418| Fat: 23g | Protein: 19g | Carbohydrates: 39g | Fiber: 5g | Sugar: 16g| Sodium: 35mg

Avocado and Yoghurt with Blueberry-Pom

Prep time: 10 minutes | Cook time: 0 minutes | Serves 2

1 cup frozen blueberries	2 tablespoons chia seeds
1 cup pomegranate seeds	1 avocado, peeled and pitted
1½ cups full-fat plain Greek yogurt	1½ cups water

1. Put the blueberries, pomegranate seeds, yogurt, chia seeds, avocado, and water in a blender.
2. Blend on high speed until smooth.
3. Divide evenly between 2 cups and enjoy!

Per Serving
Calories: 518| Fat: 31g | Protein: 22g | Carbohydrates: 42g | Fiber: 18g | Sugar: 19g| Sodium: 85mg

Collagen with Peanut Butter Cup

Prep time: 10 minutes | Cook time: 0 minutes | Serves 2

2 bananas, halved and frozen
2 tablespoons collagen powder
2 tablespoons raw

cacao powder
¼ cup peanut butter
1½ cups unsweetened almond milk

1. Put the bananas, collagen powder, cacao powder, peanut butter, and almond milk in a blender.
2. Blend on high speed until smooth.
3. Divide evenly between 2 cups and enjoy!

Per Serving
Calories: 368| Fat: 20g | Protein: 20g | Carbohydrates: 37g | Fiber: 8g | Sugar: 18g| Sodium: 183mg

Milk and Cinnamon with Cocoa Smoothie

Prep time: 15 minutes | Cook time: 0 minutes | Serves 1 to 2

¼ cup of peanut butter
½ of a medium-sized banana, sliced (if you want a cool smoothie, freeze the slices beforehand)
1 tablespoon of cocoa powder
1 cup of non-fat milk or almond milk

(chilled if you want a cool smoothie)
2 drops of vanilla extract
¼ teaspoon of cinnamon powder
2 tablespoon of ground peanuts
1 teaspoon of ground peanuts (for topping)

1. Combine all the ingredients (except the ground peanuts) into your Vitamix Blender.
2. Blend well until the mixture has a smooth consistency.
3. Pour into a glass. Sprinkle the top with the ground peanuts.
4. Do not over blend to avoid losing the nutrients.
5. Serve and drink up right away. Enjoy!

Per Serving
Calories: 349| Fat: 11g | Protein: 14g | Carbohydrates: 50g | Fiber: 3g | Sugar: 38g| Sodium: 662mg

Minty Cacao Stick Smoothie

Prep time: 10 minutes | Cook time: 0 minutes | Serves 2

1 banana, peeled
1 tablespoon coconut milk
4 spring mint
1 ½ tablespoons

cacao powder
1 apple, chopped
1 cup ice
1 cup of water

1. Add all the listed ingredients to a blender
2. Blend until you have a smooth and creamy texture
3. Serve chilled and enjoy!

Per Serving
Calories: 150| Fat: 5g | Protein: 2g | Carbohydrates: 29g | Fiber: 5g | Sugar: 18g| Sodium: 10mg

Pineapple Berry Yoghurt Shake

Prep time: 10 minutes | Cook time: 0 minutes | Serves 1 to 2

½ of a medium-sized banana, sliced (if you want a cool smoothie, freeze the slices beforehand)
1 cup of frozen yoghurt (in vanilla flavor)
½ cup of fresh pineapple chunks (frozen if you want a cool smoothie)

½ cup of raspberries (preferably fresh, but you can also use the frozen kind)
½ cup of strawberries (preferably fresh, but you can also use the frozen kind)
½ to ¾ cup of orange juice (depending on how thick you want it to be)

1. In your Vitamix Blender, combine all the ingredients together and blend until the mixture reaches a smooth consistency.
2. Do not over blend to avoid losing the nutrients.
3. Pour into a glass. Serve and drink up right away. Enjoy!

Per Serving
Calories: 290| Fat: 3g | Protein: 4g | Carbohydrates: 64g | Fiber: 5g | Sugar: 54g| Sodium: 60mg

Squash Persimmon Protein Smoothie

Prep time: 10 minutes | Cook time: 0 minutes | Serves 2

1 persimmon, topped and chopped	1 tablespoon flaxseed
1 tablespoon cinnamon	4 ounces pineapple
1 squash	1 tablespoon pea protein
	1 cup of water

1. Add all the listed ingredients to a blender
2. Blend until you have a smooth and creamy texture
3. Serve chilled and enjoy!

Per Serving
Calories: 159| Fat: 2g | Protein: 7g | Carbohydrates: 33g | Fiber: 7g | Sugar: 8g| Sodium: 12mg

Chia Chard with Berries and Cream

Prep time: 10 minutes | Cook time: 0 minutes | Serves 2

1 cup frozen mixed berries	1 cup full-fat cottage cheese
1 cup chopped chard	1½ cups unsweetened almond milk
2 tablespoons chia seeds	

1. Put the berries, chard, chia seeds, cottage cheese, and almond milk in a blender.
2. Blend on high speed until smooth.
3. Divide evenly between 2 cups and enjoy!

Per Serving
Calories: 257| Fat: 13g | Protein: 17g | Carbohydrates: 20g | Fiber: 11g | Sugar: 7g| Sodium: 572mg

Zucchini and Papaya with Toasted Coconut

Prep time: 10 minutes | Cook time: 0 minutes | Serves 2

¼ cup unsweetened shredded coconut	zucchini
1 cup frozen papaya chunks	2 scoops vanilla protein powder
1 cup chopped	1 cup coconut milk
	½ cup water

1. Preheat the oven to 350°F.
2. Spread the shredded coconut on a baking sheet and bake in the oven for 3 to 6 minutes, or until lightly toasted. Let it cool to room temperature.
3. Put the toasted coconut, papaya, zucchini, protein powder, coconut milk, and water in a blender. Blend on high speed until smooth.
4. Divide evenly between 2 cups and enjoy!

Per Serving
Calories: 378| Fat: 29g | Protein: 16g | Carbohydrates: 17g | Fiber: 3g | Sugar: 10g| Sodium: 76mg

Fruity Yoghurt and Avocado Blend

Prep time: 15 minutes | Cook time: 0 minutes | Serves 1 to 2

½ cup of avocado (preferably fresh and organic)	½ cup of non-fat Greek yoghurt
¼ cup of pineapple chunks (frozen if you want a cool smoothie)	2 tablespoons of goji berries (optional)
¼ cup of mango, cubed (frozen if you want a cool smoothie)	1 cup of coconut water (chilled)
½ cup of romaine lettuce	1 tablespoon of coconut flakes
½ cup of spinach	2 tablespoons of honey or agave nectar (for sweetening)

1. Wilt the spinach using steam or in a pan. Set aside for it to cool.
2. In your Vitamix Blender, combine the spinach, romaine lettuce, and coconut water. Blend well until the greens are properly broken down.
3. Add in the rest of the ingredients (except half of the coconut flakes) and blend until the mixture is smooth in consistency.
4. Add in some honey or agave nectar and give the mixture two to three more pulses.
5. Pour into a glass. Sprinkle the top with coconut flakes. Do not over blend to avoid losing the nutrients.
6. Serve and drink up right away. Enjoy!

Per Serving
Calories: 235| Fat: 27g | Protein: 6g | Carbohydrates: 96g | Fiber: 9g | Sugar: 57g| Sodium: 494mg

Watermelon with Beet and Yoghurt

Prep time: 10 minutes | Cook time: 0 minutes | Serves 2

1 cup cubed watermelon, frozen	1 cup full-fat plain Greek yogurt
½ cup frozen raspberries	2 scoops protein powder
½ cup chopped red beets	¾ cup water

1. Put the watermelon, raspberries, beets, yogurt, protein powder, and water in a blender.
2. Blend on high speed until smooth.
3. Divide evenly between 2 cups and enjoy!

Per Serving
Calories: 220| Fat: 7g | Protein: 23g | Carbohydrates: 13g | Fiber: 3g | Sugar: 8g| Sodium: 97mg

Cucumber Hemp with Vanilla Revive

Prep time: 10 minutes | Cook time: 0 minutes | Serves 2

1 cup frozen pitted cherries	3 tablespoons hulled hemp seeds
1 banana, halved and frozen	2 scoops vanilla protein powder
½ cup chopped cucumber	1½ cups water

1. Put the cherries, banana, cucumber, hemp seeds, protein powder, and water in a blender.
2. Blend on high speed until smooth.
3. Divide evenly between 2 cups and enjoy!

Per Serving
Calories: 237| Fat: 9g | Protein: 19g | Carbohydrates: 24g | Fiber: 3g | Sugar: 14g| Sodium: 24mg

Milky Dandelion with Blueberry-Oat

Prep time: 10 minutes | Cook time: 0 minutes | Serves 2

1 cup frozen blueberries	½ cup rolled oats
1 cup chopped dandelion greens	3 tablespoons peanut butter
	1½ cups whole milk

1. Put the blueberries, dandelion greens, oats, peanut butter, and milk in a blender.
2. Blend on high speed until smooth.
3. Divide evenly between 2 cups and enjoy!

Per Serving
Calories: 446| Fat: 20g | Protein: 19g | Carbohydrates: 51g | Fiber: 9g | Sugar: 18g| Sodium: 94mg

Grapy Spinach with Berry Yoghurt

Prep time: 10 minutes | Cook time: 0 minutes | Serves 2

½ cup frozen red grapes	4 tablespoons peanut butter
½ cup frozen mixed berries	1 cup full-fat plain Greek yogurt
1 cup fresh spinach	½ cup water

1. Put the grapes, berries, spinach, peanut butter, yogurt, and water in a blender.
2. Blend on high speed until smooth.
3. Divide evenly between 2 cups and enjoy!

Per Serving
Calories: 342| Fat: 23g | Protein: 19g | Carbohydrates: 18g | Fiber: 4g | Sugar: 11g| Sodium: 90mg

Kale with Yoghurt Ginger-Plum

Prep time: 10 minutes | Cook time: 0 minutes | Serves 2

3 plums, diced and frozen	2 scoops protein powder
1 cup chopped kale	1 cup full-fat plain Greek yogurt
1 (1-inch) piece ginger, sliced	¾ cup water

1. Put the plums, kale, ginger, protein powder, yogurt, and water in a blender.
2. Blend on high speed until smooth.
3. Divide evenly between 2 cups and enjoy!

Per Serving
Calories: 220| Fat: 7g | Protein: 24g | Carbohydrates: 13g | Fiber: 2g | Sugar: 10g| Sodium: 107mg

Mango with Beets and Protein

Prep time: 10 minutes | Cook time: 0 minutes | Serves 2

2 medium oranges, peeled	golden beets
½ cup frozen mango chunks	2 scoops protein powder
½ cup chopped	1½ cups coconut water

1. Put the oranges, mango, beets, protein powder, and coconut water in a blender.
2. Blend on high speed until smooth.
3. Divide evenly between 2 cups and enjoy!

Per Serving
Calories: 204| Fat: 2g | Protein: 16g | Carbohydrates: 34g | Fiber: 7g | Sugar: 25g| Sodium: 240mg

Milky Beet and Cherry Smoothie

Prep time: 10 minutes | Cook time: 0 minutes | Serves 1 to 2

1 cup of beets, peeled and cut into slices (preferably fresh and organic)	½ cup cherries (preferably fresh, but you can also use the frozen and canned kind)
½ of a small sized banana, sliced (if you want a cool smoothie, freeze the slices beforehand)	1 cup of non-fat milk
	¼ teaspoon of salt
	3 tablespoons of honey or maple syrup

1. Cook the beets slices using steam (this will retain the nutrients in them, unlike in boiling) until they are tender enough.
2. Set aside to let them cool.
3. In your Vitamix Blender, combine all the ingredients and blend until the mixture is smooth in consistency.
4. Do not over blend to avoid losing the nutrients.
5. Pour into a glass. Serve and drink up right away. Enjoy!

Per Serving
Calories: 266| Fat: 3g | Protein: 3g | Carbohydrates: 51g | Fiber: 4g | Sugar: 43g| Sodium: 661mg

Chapter 9: Drinkable Snacks and Desserts

Berry and Yoghurt Beets

Prep time: 10 minutes | Cook time: 0 minutes | Serves 2

½ cup frozen pitted cherries
¼ cup frozen blueberries
¼ cup frozen blackberries

½ cup chopped red beets
½ cup full-fat plain Greek yogurt
1½ cups water

1. Put the cherries, blueberries, blackberries, beets, yogurt, and water in a blender.
2. Blend on high speed until smooth.
3. Divide evenly between 2 cups and enjoy!

Per Serving
Calories: 207| Fat: 7g | Protein: 12g | Carbohydrates: 23g | Fiber: 6g | Sugar: 16g| Sodium: 102mg

Limey Grape Juice

Prep time: 5 minutes | Cook time: 0 minutes | Serves 1

1 pink grapefruit, peeled, sliced
2 celery stalks, chopped

1 red pepper, cored, stem removed
½ lime, skin removed

1. Add liquid first, then softer ingredients and harder items like ice or frozen fruit last.
2. Blend on medium and increase to high for 1 minute.
3. Repeat as necessary.

Per Serving
Calories: 111| Fat: 1g | Protein: 3g | Carbohydrates: 28g | Fiber: 4g | Sugar: 21g| Sodium: 32mg

Minty Grapefruit Juice

Prep time: 5 minutes | Cook time: 0 minutes | Serves 1

2 grapefruits, peeled and sectioned to fit into the juicer

8-10 leaves of fresh mint

1. Add liquid first, then softer ingredients and harder items like ice or frozen fruit last.
2. Blend on medium and increase to high for 1 minute.
3. Repeat as necessary.

Per Serving
Calories: 164| Fat: 1g | Protein: 3g | Carbohydrates: 41g | Fiber: 6g | Sugar: 36g| Sodium: 0mg

Radish Blueberry Blast

Prep time: 10 minutes | Cook time: 0 minutes | Serves 2

1 cup frozen blueberries
1 pear, chopped
1 banana, halved and frozen

1 cup chopped radishes
1½ cups unsweetened almond milk

1. Put the blueberries, pear, banana, radishes, and almond milk in a blender.
2. Blend on high speed until smooth.
3. Divide evenly between 2 cups and enjoy!

Per Serving
Calories: 153| Fat: 3g | Protein: 2g | Carbohydrates: 32g | Fiber: 8g | Sugar: 19g| Sodium: 144mg

Limeade Cucumber with Cherry

Prep time: 10 minutes | Cook time: 0 minutes | Serves 2

1 cup frozen pitted cherries
1 lime, peeled
½ cup fresh spinach

½ cup chopped cucumber
1½ cups coconut water

1. Put the cherries, lime, spinach, cucumber, and coconut water in a blender.
2. Blend on high speed until smooth.
3. Divide evenly between 2 cups and enjoy!

Per Serving
Calories: 86| Fat: 1g | Protein: 3g | Carbohydrates: 20g | Fiber: 4.3g | Sugar: 12g| Sodium: 209mg

Pineapple and Peach Zinc Defense

Prep time: 10 minutes | Cook time: 0 minutes | Serves 2

½ cup frozen sliced peaches
½ cup frozen pineapple chunks
1 cup fresh spinach
½ cup pumpkin seeds
1 cup plain kefir
½ cup water

1. Put the peaches, pineapple, spinach, pumpkin seeds, kefir, and water in a blender.
2. Blend on high speed until smooth.
3. Divide evenly between 2 cups and enjoy!

Per Serving
Calories: 186| Fat: 7g | Protein: 8g | Carbohydrates: 25g | Fiber: 1g | Sugar: 13g| Sodium: 98mg

Turmeric and Cauliflower with Mango

Prep time: 10 minutes | Cook time: 0 minutes | Serves 2

1 cup frozen mango chunks
1 cup frozen cauliflower florets
2 teaspoons ground turmeric
2 tablespoons ground flaxseed
1 cup full-fat plain Greek yogurt
1½ cups water

1. Put the mango, cauliflower, turmeric, flaxseed, yogurt, and water in a blender.
2. Blend on high speed until smooth.
3. Divide evenly between 2 cups and enjoy!

Per Serving
Calories: 222| Fat: 10g | Protein: 22g | Carbohydrates: 20g | Fiber: 5g | Sugar: 14g| Sodium: 68mg

Coconut with Strawberry-Hibiscus

Prep time: 10 minutes | Cook time: 0 minutes | Serves 2

1 tablespoon dried hibiscus flowers
½ cup boiling water
1 cup frozen strawberries
1 banana, halved and frozen
1 cup chopped cauliflower
1 cup coconut water

1. Steep the hibiscus flowers in the boiling water for 5 minutes.
2. Allow the tea to cool to room temperature, without removing the hibiscus flowers.
3. Alternatively, you can prepare the tea ahead of time and chill it in the refrigerator for up to 5 days.
4. Once the tea is cooled, pour the tea with the soaked hibiscus flowers, strawberries, banana, cauliflower, and coconut water into a blender.
5. Blend on high speed until smooth.
6. Divide evenly between 2 cups and enjoy!

Per Serving
Calories: 128| Fat: 1g | Protein: 3g | Carbohydrates: 30g | Fiber: 8g | Sugar: 16g| Sodium: 143mg

Chard and Cashew Berry Sage

Prep time: 10 minutes | Cook time: 0 minutes | Serves 2

1 cup frozen blackberries
1 cup chopped chard
½ cup raw cashews
1 teaspoon vanilla extract
6 fresh sage leaves
1½ cups water

1. Put the blackberries, chard, cashews, vanilla, sage, and water in a blender.
2. Blend on high speed until smooth.
3. Divide evenly between 2 cups and enjoy!

Per Serving
Calories: 196| Fat: 13g | Protein: 7g | Carbohydrates: 18g | Fiber: 5g | Sugar: 6g| Sodium: 43mg

Pumpkin Chai

Prep time: 10 minutes | Cook time: 0 minutes | Serves 2

½ cup pumpkin puree
1 banana, halved and frozen
½ teaspoon pumpkin spice blend
1 teaspoon vanilla extract
1½ cups unsweetened almond milk

1. Put the pumpkin puree, banana, pumpkin spice blend, vanilla, and almond milk in a blender. Blend on high speed until smooth.
2. Divide evenly between 2 cups and enjoy!

Per Serving
Calories: 157| Fat: 6g | Protein: 4g | Carbohydrates: 23g | Fiber: 2g | Sugar: 7g| Sodium: 124mg

Spicy Spinach with Pear and Kiwi

Prep time: 10 minutes | Cook time: 0 minutes | Serves 2

1 pear, chopped and frozen
1 kiwi, peeled, chopped, and frozen
1 cup fresh spinach
¼ teaspoon cayenne pepper
1½ cups unsweetened almond milk

1. Put the pear, kiwi, spinach, cayenne pepper, and almond milk in a blender.
2. Blend on high speed until smooth.
3. Divide evenly between 2 cups and enjoy!

Per Serving
Calories: 167| Fat: 5g | Protein: 4g | Carbohydrates: 29g | Fiber: 5g | Sugar: 17g| Sodium: 316mg

Minty Cucumber with Chia and Watermelon

Prep time: 10 minutes | Cook time: 0 minutes | Serves 2

1 cup cubed watermelon, frozen
1 cup chopped cucumber, frozen
¼ cup lightly packed fresh mint leaves
1 tablespoon chia seeds
1 cup full-fat plain Greek yogurt
¾ cup water

1. Put the watermelon, cucumber, mint, chia seeds, yogurt, and water in a blender.
2. Blend on high speed until smooth.
3. Divide evenly between 2 cups and enjoy!

Per Serving
Calories: 191| Fat: 9g | Protein: 13g | Carbohydrates: 13g | Fiber: 5g | Sugar: 6g| Sodium: 52mg

Jicama with almond Milk

Prep time: 10 minutes | Cook time: 0 minutes | Serves 2

½ cup frozen strawberries
1 cup chopped jicama
½ cup frozen
blueberries
¼ cup almonds
1½ cups almond milk

1. Put the strawberries, jicama, blueberries, almonds, and almond milk in a blender.

2. Blend on high speed until smooth.
3. Divide evenly between 2 cups and enjoy!

Per Serving
Calories: 184| Fat: 12g | Protein: 5g | Carbohydrates: 17g | Fiber: 8g | Sugar: 7g| Sodium: 123mg

Tropical Matcha

Prep time: 10 minutes | Cook time: 0 minutes | Serves 2

½ cup frozen papaya chunks
½ cup frozen mango chunks
1 cup chopped kale
2 teaspoons matcha powder
1 avocado, peeled and pitted
1½ cups water

1. Put the papaya, mango, kale, matcha powder, avocado, and water in a blender.
2. Blend on high speed until smooth.
3. Divide evenly between 2 cups and enjoy!

Per Serving
Calories: 218| Fat: 15g | Protein: 4g | Carbohydrates: 22g | Fiber: 9g | Sugar: 9g| Sodium: 23mg

Kale and Celery Green Juice

Prep time: 10 minutes | Cook time: 0 minutes | Serves 2

3 handfuls of kale (or about 3 loosely packed cups)
1 whole apple, cored and cut into large chunks
1 stalk of celery, cut into large chunks
½ English cucumber, cut into large chunks
Juice from ½ a lime
1 handful of parsley or about 1 cup loosely packed
1 cup water
Ice

1. Add liquid first, then softer ingredients and harder items like ice or frozen fruit last.
2. Blend on medium and increase to high for 1 minute.
3. Repeat as necessary.

Per Serving
Calories: 711| Fat: 10g | Protein: 44g | Carbohydrates: 145g | Fiber: 30g | Sugar: 13g| Sodium: 1,076mg

Ginger and Almond Beets with Carrot

Prep time: 10 minutes | Cook time: 0 minutes | Serves 2

1 green apple, chopped and frozen
½ cup chopped red beets, frozen
1 cup chopped carrots
1 (1-inch) piece ginger, sliced
1½ cups unsweetened almond milk

1. Put the apple, beets, carrots, ginger, and almond milk in a blender. Blend on high speed until smooth.
2. Divide evenly between 2 cups and enjoy!

Per Serving
Calories: 103| Fat: 3g | Protein: 2g | Carbohydrates: 20g | Fiber: 4g | Sugar: 13g| Sodium: 172mg

Yoghurt and Banana-Zucchini Bread

Prep time: 10 minutes | Cook time: 0 minutes | Serves 2

1 cup chopped zucchini
2 bananas, halved and frozen
¼ cup walnuts
½ teaspoon ground cinnamon
1 cup full-fat plain yogurt
1½ cups water

1. Put the zucchini, bananas, walnuts, cinnamon, yogurt, and water in a blender.
2. Blend on high speed until smooth.
3. Divide evenly between 2 cups and enjoy!

Per Serving
Calories: 287| Fat: 14g | Protein: 9g | Carbohydrates: 37g | Fiber: 5g | Sugar: 21g| Sodium: 64mg

Layered Berries and Cream

Prep time: 10 minutes | Cook time: 0 minutes | Serves 2

1 cup full-fat plain Greek yogurt
1 teaspoon honey
½ teaspoon vanilla extract
1½ cups whole milk, divided
2 cups frozen mixed berries

1. To prepare the bottom cream layer: Put the yogurt, honey, vanilla, and ½ cup of milk in a blender. Blend on high speed until smooth.
2. Divide the "cream" evenly between 2 cups. Set aside.
3. To prepare the berry layer: Put the mixed berries and remaining 1 cup of milk in the blender. Blend on high speed until smooth.
4. Pour the berry layer carefully over the cream layer, dividing evenly between 2 cups. Enjoy!

Per Serving
Calories: 238| Fat: 10g | Protein: 11g | Carbohydrates: 29g | Fiber: 3g | Sugar: 25g| Sodium: 125mg

Guava and Orange Jicama Punch

Prep time: 10 minutes | Cook time: 0 minutes | Serves 2

1 medium orange, peeled
1 cup chopped, seeded guava, frozen
½ cup diced jicama
1 cup chopped kale
1 cup plain kefir
½ cup water

1. Put the orange, guava, jicama, kale, kefir, and water in a blender.
2. Blend on high speed until smooth.
3. Divide evenly between 2 cups and enjoy!

Per Serving
Calories: 198| Fat: 5g | Protein: 8g | Carbohydrates: 33g | Fiber: 8g | Sugar: 19g| Sodium: 19mg

Milky Chia Berry-Basil

Prep time: 10 minutes | Cook time: 0 minutes | Serves 2

1 cup frozen mixed berries
1 cup chopped chard
¼ cup lightly packed fresh basil
1 tablespoon chia seeds
1½ cups unsweetened almond milk

1. Put the berries, chard, basil, chia seeds, and almond milk in a blender.
2. Blend on high speed until smooth.
3. Divide evenly between 2 cups and enjoy!

Per Serving
Calories: 212| Fat: 12g | Protein: 7g | Carbohydrates: 24g | Fiber: 13g | Sugar: 8g| Sodium: 322mg

Grapy Zucchini with Citrus Crush

Prep time: 10 minutes | Cook time: 0 minutes | Serves 2

1 medium orange, peeled	pineapple chunks
½ medium grapefruit, peeled	½ cup chopped zucchini
½ cup frozen	½ cup coconut milk
	½ cup water

1. Put the orange, grapefruit, pineapple, zucchini, coconut milk, and water in a blender.
2. Blend on high speed until smooth.
3. Divide evenly between 2 cups and enjoy!

Per Serving
Calories: 197| Fat: 12g | Protein: 3g | Carbohydrates: 23g | Fiber: 3g | Sugar: 15g| Sodium: 12mg

Carrot and Orange with Coconut Milk

Prep time: 10 minutes | Cook time: 0 minutes | Serves 2

2 oranges, peeled	carrots
1 banana, halved and frozen	¼ cup raw cashews
½ cup chopped	½ cup coconut milk
	1 cup water

1. Put the oranges, banana, carrots, cashews, coconut milk, and water in a blender.
2. Blend on high speed until smooth.
3. Divide evenly between 2 cups and enjoy!

Per Serving
Calories: 265| Fat: 14g | Protein: 4g | Carbohydrates: 36g | Fiber: 6g | Sugar: 21g| Sodium: 39mg

Cheesy Strawberry Hemp

Prep time: 10 minutes | Cook time: 0 minutes | Serves 2

2 cups frozen strawberries	3 tablespoons hulled hemp seeds
½ cup full-fat cottage cheese	½ cup full-fat plain yogurt
2 pitted dates	1½ cups water

1. Put the strawberries, cottage cheese, dates, hemp seeds, yogurt, and water in a blender.
2. Blend on high speed until smooth.
3. Divide evenly between 2 cups and enjoy!

Per Serving
Calories: 293| Fat: 12g | Protein: 15g | Carbohydrates: 35g | Fiber: 5g | Sugar: 28g| Sodium: 236mg

Turmeric with Yoghurt and Lemon Tart

Prep time: 10 minutes | Cook time: 0 minutes | Serves 2

1 lemon, peeled	1 teaspoon ground turmeric
2 bananas, halved and frozen	1 cup full-fat plain yogurt
2 tablespoons chia seeds	1½ cups water

1. Put the lemon, bananas, chia seeds, turmeric, yogurt, and water in a blender.
2. Blend on high speed until smooth.
3. Divide evenly between 2 cups and enjoy!

Per Serving
Calories: 300| Fat: 10g | Protein: 9g | Carbohydrates: 50g | Fiber: 13g | Sugar: 22g| Sodium: 63mg

Garlic and Tabasco Juice

Prep time: 15 minutes | Cook time: 0 minutes | Serves 2

1 tablespoon extra virgin olive oil	1 tablespoon honey
5 medium-large tomatoes, chopped	1 dash tabasco sauce
½ onion, chopped	1 dash Worcestershire sauce
2 cloves garlic	salt & pepper
1 beet, chopped	2 small cucumbers, chopped
1 carrot, chopped	¼ cup fresh parsley

1. Add liquid first, then softer ingredients and harder items like ice or frozen fruit last.
2. Blend on medium and increase to high for 1 minute.
3. Repeat as necessary.

Per Serving
Calories: 518| Fat: 31g | Protein: 22g | Carbohydrates: 42g | Fiber: 18g | Sugar: 19g| Sodium: 85mg

Peachy Cinnamon Cobbler

Prep time: 10 minutes | Cook time: 0 minutes | Serves 2

2 cups frozen sliced peaches
½ cup rolled oats
½ teaspoon ground cinnamon
2 tablespoons ground flaxseed
1½ cups unsweetened almond milk

1. Put the peaches, oats, cinnamon, flaxseed, and almond milk in a blender.
2. Blend on high speed until smooth.
3. Divide evenly between 2 cups and enjoy!

Per Serving
Calories: 277| Fat: 8g | Protein: 10g | Carbohydrates: 44g | Fiber: 9g | Sugar: 13g| Sodium: 123mg

Avocado and Banana with Chocolate Chip

Prep time: 10 minutes | Cook time: 0 minutes | Serves 2

2 bananas, halved and frozen
1 avocado, peeled and pitted
1 tablespoon raw cacao powder
1½ cups unsweetened almond milk
2 tablespoons cacao nibs

1. Put the bananas, avocado, cacao powder, and almond milk in a blender. Blend on high speed until smooth.
2. Add the cacao nibs to the blender bowl. Using a spatula, fold them into the smoothie until combined.
3. Divide evenly between 2 cups and enjoy!

Per Serving
Calories: 263| Fat: 25g | Protein: 5g | Carbohydrates: 15g | Fiber: 11g | Sugar: 1g| Sodium: 131mg

Berry with Pomegranate Sorbet

Prep time: 10 minutes | Cook time: 0 minutes | Serves 2

1½ cups frozen pomegranate seeds
½ cup frozen raspberries
1 banana, halved and frozen
1 tablespoon chia seeds
1 cup full-fat plain yogurt
1½ cups water

1. Put the pomegranate seeds, raspberries, banana, chia seeds, yogurt, and water in a blender.
2. Blend on high speed until smooth.
3. Divide evenly between 2 cups and enjoy!

Per Serving
Calories: 266| Fat: 7g | Protein: 7g | Carbohydrates: 49g | Fiber: 13g | Sugar: 29g| Sodium: 35mg

Almond and Banana with Pistachio Cream

Prep time: 10 minutes | Cook time: 0 minutes | Serves 2

⅓ cup raw pistachios
1 banana, halved and frozen
½ avocado, chopped and frozen
1 teaspoon vanilla extract
1½ cups unsweetened almond milk

1. Put the pistachios, banana, avocado, vanilla, and almond milk in a blender.
2. Blend on high speed until smooth.
3. Divide evenly between 2 cups and enjoy!

Per Serving
Calories: 271 Fat: 19g | Protein: 7g | Carbohydrates: 24g | Fiber: 8g | Sugar: 9g| Sodium: 124mg

Cashew with Caramel-Covered Apple

Prep time: 10 minutes | Cook time: 0 minutes | Serves 2

2 apples, chopped and frozen
2 pitted dates
¼ cup raw cashews
2 tablespoons collagen powder
1½ cups unsweetened almond milk

1. Put the apples, dates, cashews, collagen powder, and almond milk in a blender.
2. Blend on high speed until smooth.
3. Divide evenly between 2 cups and enjoy!

Per Serving
Calories: 300| Fat: 9g | Protein: 13g | Carbohydrates: 49g | Fiber: 7g | Sugar: 35g| Sodium: 179mg

Raspberries and White Chocolate

Prep time: 10 minutes | Cook time: 0 minutes | Serves 2

1 cup frozen raspberries
1 banana, halved and frozen
2 tablespoons coconut
butter
½ teaspoon vanilla extract
1½ cups milk

1. Put the raspberries, banana, coconut butter, vanilla, and milk in a blender.
2. Blend on high speed until smooth.
3. Divide evenly between 2 cups and enjoy!

Per Serving
Calories: 256| Fat: 15g | Protein: 7g | Carbohydrates: 25g | Fiber: 2g | Sugar: 17g| Sodium: 73mg

Lemony Celery and Parsley Green Juice

Prep time: 10 minutes | Cook time: 0 minutes | Serves 2

1 ½ cups water
2 cups kale
2 green apples, cored
½ cup parsley leaves
1 medium cucumber, quartered
2 celery stalks, roughly chopped
1 (1-inch) piece of ginger, peeled
2 tablespoons lemon juice

1. Add liquid first, then softer ingredients and harder items like ice or frozen fruit last.
2. Blend on medium and increase to high for 1 minute.
3. Repeat as necessary.

Per Serving
Calories: 127| Fat: 0g | Protein: 2g | Carbohydrates: 31g | Fiber: 6g | Sugar: 21g| Sodium: 36mg

Beets and Carrot with Orange Juice

Prep time: 5 minutes | Cook time: 0 minutes | Serves 1

5 peeled carrots
1 bunch beet greens (about 5-6 large), can also use chard
2 small oranges, peeled and and cut
into half through the equator, seeds removed
2 apples, cut into quarters, cores removed

1. Add liquid first, then softer ingredients and harder items like ice or frozen fruit last.
2. Blend on medium and increase to high for 1 minute.
3. Repeat as necessary.

Per Serving
Calories: 459| Fat: 2g | Protein: 7g | Carbohydrates: 116g | Fiber: 25g | Sugar: 76g| Sodium: 2,074mg

Coconut Butter and Cherry Pudding

Prep time: 10 minutes | Cook time: 0 minutes | Serves 2

1 cup frozen pitted cherries
1 cup frozen cauliflower florets
1 cup full-fat plain
yogurt
1 tablespoon coconut butter (or coconut manna)
1½ cups whole milk

1. Put the cherries, cauliflower, yogurt, coconut butter, and milk in a blender.
2. Blend on high speed until smooth.
3. Divide evenly between 2 cups and enjoy!

Per Serving
Calories: 274| Fat: 14g | Protein: 11g | Carbohydrates: 27g | Fiber: 5g | Sugar: 23g| Sodium: 142mg

Cinnamon and Almond Milk with Eggnog

Prep time: 10 minutes | Cook time: 0 minutes | Serves 2

2 bananas, halved and frozen
2 pitted dates
½ teaspoon ground nutmeg
½ teaspoon ground cinnamon
1½ cups unsweetened almond milk

1. Put the bananas, dates, nutmeg, cinnamon, and almond milk in a blender.
2. Blend on high speed until smooth.
3. Divide evenly between 2 cups and enjoy!

Per Serving
Calories: 202| Fat: 3g | Protein: 3g | Carbohydrates: 46g | Fiber: 6g | Sugar: 31g| Sodium: 122mg

Grape and Cucumber Green Juice

Prep time: 10 minutes | Cook time: 0 minutes | Serves 1

2 cups baby spinach {packed full}
½ English cucumber, peeled
3 fuji apples

2 navel oranges
1 ruby red grapefruit
1 small lemon, peeled {optional}

1. Add liquid first, then softer ingredients and harder items like ice or frozen fruit last.
2. Blend on medium and increase to high for 1 minute.
3. Repeat as necessary.

Per Serving
Calories: 312| Fat: 2g | Protein: 9g | Carbohydrates: 76g | Fiber: 17g | Sugar: 51g| Sodium: 694mg

Squash and Dates Butter Pecan

Prep time: 10 minutes | Cook time: 0 minutes | Serves 2

½ cup frozen butternut squash chunks
1 banana, halved and frozen

2 pitted dates
¼ cup pecans
1½ cups unsweetened almond milk

1. Put the squash, banana, dates, pecans, and almond milk in a blender.
2. Blend on high speed until smooth.
3. Divide evenly between 2 cups and enjoy!

Per Serving
Calories: 255| Fat: 12g | Protein: 3g | Carbohydrates: 38g | Fiber: 6g | Sugar: 24g| Sodium: 122mg

Organic Raspberry and Cucumber Juice

Prep time: 5 minutes | Cook time: 0 minutes | Serves 1

5 carrots
1 pear
12 ounces of organic

raspberries
1 cucumber

1. Add liquid first, then softer ingredients and harder items like ice or frozen fruit last.

2. Blend on medium and increase to high for 1 minute.
3. Repeat as necessary.

Per Serving
Calories: 428| Fat: 3g | Protein: 18g | Carbohydrates: 101g | Fiber: 38g | Sugar: 50g| Sodium: 220mg

Apple and Ginger Carrot Juice

Prep time: 5 minutes | Cook time: 0 minutes | Serves 1

3 organic carrots
1 apple
½ inch piece of ginger

a few sprigs of parsley

1. Add liquid first, then softer ingredients and harder items like ice or frozen fruit last.
2. Blend on medium and increase to high for 1 minute.
3. Repeat as necessary.

Per Serving
Calories: 170| Fat: 1g | Protein: 2g | Carbohydrates: 43g | Fiber: 10g | Sugar: 28g| Sodium: 129mg

Lemon and Ginger Green Power Juice

Prep time: 10 minutes | Cook time: 0 minutes | Serves 1

6 large fuji or gala apples, quartered
4 cups baby spinach leaves

1 bunch of parsley
2 inches fresh ginger, skin removed
1 lemon

1. Add liquid first, then softer ingredients and harder items like ice or frozen fruit last.
2. Blend on medium and increase to high for 1 minute.
3. Repeat as necessary.

Per Serving
Calories: 369| Fat: 1g | Protein: 4g | Carbohydrates: 97g | Fiber: 1g | Sugar: 70g| Sodium: 55mg

Appendix 1: Measurement Conversion Chart

VOLUME EQUIVALENTS(DRY)

US STANDARD	METRIC (APPROXIMATE)
1/8 teaspoon	0.5 mL
1/4 teaspoon	1 mL
1/2 teaspoon	2 mL
3/4 teaspoon	4 mL
1 teaspoon	5 mL
1 tablespoon	15 mL
1/4 cup	59 mL
1/2 cup	118 mL
3/4 cup	177 mL
1 cup	235 mL
2 cups	475 mL
3 cups	700 mL
4 cups	1 L

VOLUME EQUIVALENTS(LIQUID)

US STANDARD	US STANDARD (OUNCES)	METRIC (APPROXIMATE)
2 tablespoons	1 fl.oz.	30 mL
1/4 cup	2 fl.oz.	60 mL
1/2 cup	4 fl.oz.	120 mL
1 cup	8 fl.oz.	240 mL
1 1/2 cup	12 fl.oz.	355 mL
2 cups or 1 pint	16 fl.oz.	475 mL
4 cups or 1 quart	32 fl.oz.	1 L
1 gallon	128 fl.oz.	4 L

TEMPERATURES EQUIVALENTS

FAHRENHEIT(F)	CELSIUS(C) (APPROXIMATE)
225 °F	107 °C
250 °F	120 °C
275 °F	135 °C
300 °F	150 °C
325 °F	160 °C
350 °F	180 °C
375 °F	190 °C
400 °F	205 °C
425 °F	220 °C
450 °F	235 °C
475 °F	245 °C
500 °F	260 °C

WEIGHT EQUIVALENTS

US STANDARD	METRIC (APPROXIMATE)
1 ounce	28 g
2 ounces	57 g
5 ounces	142 g
10 ounces	284 g
15 ounces	425 g
16 ounces (1 pound)	455 g
1.5 pounds	680 g
2 pounds	907 g

Appendix 2: Recipe Index

A

Almond and Banana with Pistachio Cream 88
Almond and Mango with Honey Smoothie   73
Almond and Peach Oat 18
Almond Berry Smoothie   22
Almond Milk and Honey Smoothie 21
Almond Pumpkin Pie 38
Almond with Anti-Aging Cacao   58
Almond with Kale and Banana Power Protein 76
Almond-Banana-Oat Recovery 75
Almond-Chia Smoothie Bowl 18
Anti-Aging Turmeric Smoothie 52
Apple and Ginger Carrot Juice 90
Apple and Kiwi Green Goblin   75
Apple and Milky Raisin Oat 19
Apple Cider Detox Remedy Drink 64
Apple with Chia Seed Smoothie 41
Avocado and Apple Green Goodness   46
Avocado and Banana with Chocolate Chip 88
Avocado and Berry Nice   54
Avocado and Yoghurt with Blueberry-Pom 77
Avocado Green Superfood Smoothie 42
Avocado with Kale and Coconut Milk 17
Avocado with Pineapple Smoothie 18

B

Banana and Almond Relaxing Oatmeal 56
Banana and Apple Berry Smoothie 25
Banana and Cacao Superfood Smoothie 27
Banana and Chocolate Malt Superfood Smoothie 27
Banana and Green Tea 35
Banana and Limey Strawberry Smoothie 39
Banana and Pumpkin Power Smoothie 76
Banana Berry with Blue Ginger 65
Banana Flaxseed Oat with Yoghurt 21
Banana Medjool Energy Smoothie 71
Banana with Kale and Coconut Delight 31
Banana-Almond-Chia 22
Beets and Carrot with Orange Juice 89
Berry and Avocado Anti-Wrinkle Smoothie 57
Berry and Melon Perfection 49
Berry and Minty Coconut with Lemon 55
Berry and Yoghurt Beets 83
Berry Flaxseed with Dates 68
Berry Mint Superfood Smoothie 25
Berry Spinach and Apple Pie Smoothie   39
Berry Spinach Green Smoothie 44
Berry Spirulina with Avocado 65
Berry with Green Vanilla Smoothie 41
Berry with Pomegranate Sorbet 88
Berry with Sweet Pea Smoothie   30
Berry Yoghurt with Energy Superfood 76
Black Pepper and Pineapple Smoothie 32

Blueberry Almond Butter Smoothies 71
Blueberry Fruit Detox Smoothie 60
Blueberry Ultimate Diet Smoothie 31
Blueberry with Mango Superfood Smoothie 27
Buttered Berry and Banana Smoothie   38
Buttered Maca Smoothie 25
Buttered Vanilla Yoghurt 33

C-D

Cantaloupe Berry Oat 20
Carrot and Apple Hot Tomato 49
Carrot and Banana Crisp Apple Smoothie 42
Carrot and Orange with Coconut Milk 87
Carrot and Strawberry Oatmeal   50
Carrot and Turmeric Antioxidant Smoothie 53
Carrot Hemp Green Smoothie Bowl 45
Carrot Spring Cleaning Detox 66
Cashew with Caramel-Covered Apple 88
Cashew with Vanilla Apple Pie   46
Cauliflower with Raspberry and Chia 74
Celery Mango Super Cleanse 65
Chard and Cashew Berry Sage 84
Cheesy Almond and Banana Cream   32
Cheesy Almond Milk with Avocado   20
Cheesy Strawberry Hemp 87
Cherry Protein and Coconut Smoothie 73
Chia and Banana Strawberry Peach   35
Chia Berry Anti-Aging Superfood   54
Chia Chard with Berries and Cream 79
Chia Cherry Yoghurt 20
Chia Espresso with Vanilla Yoghurt   49
Chia with Berry Carrot   32
Chia with Pineapple and Mango   56
Chocolatey Minty Spinach   33
Chocolatey Spunky Monkey   35
Cilantro Algae with Kale 66
Cinnamon and Almond Milk with Eggnog 89
Cinnamon and Honey Smoothie   22
Cinnamon Banana Pumpkin   33
Cinnamon Raisin Bliss   31
Cinnamon with Kale Power Detox Smoothie 64
Cinnamon Yoghurt Energy Boost Smoothie 73
Citrus with Chia Seeds Smoothie   24
Clementine with Carrot Detox Smoothie 61
Cocoa Mocha Milk Shake   19
Coconut Butter and Cherry Pudding 89
Coconut Delight with Anti-Aging Turmeric   56
Coconut Flakes with Pineapple 19
Coconut Milk and Egg Smoothie 18
Coconut with Strawberry-Hibiscus 84
Collagen with Peanut Butter Cup 78
Creamy Berry and Coconut Shake 68
Creamy Berry Smoothie   39

Creamy Blueberry Bliss   37
Creamy Xanthan and Strawberry Smoothie   72
Cucumber Celery Cranberry   67
Cucumber Hemp with Vanilla Revive   80
Cucumber with Spinach and Orange Smoothie   74
Divine Chocolate Milk   32

F-G

Flaxseed and Orange Anti-Ultra Violet   58
Flaxseed Green and Berry Smoothie   43
Fruity Detox Special   68
Fruity Energy Boost Smoothie   71
Fruity Flax Seeds Smoothie   38
Fruity Grab Bag   48
Fruity Kale and Lemon Smoothie   46
Fruity Yoghurt and Avocado Blend   79
Garlic and Tabasco Juice   87
Ginger and Almond Beets with Carrot   86
Ginger and Pineapple Antioxidant Refresher   73
Ginger and Strawberry Deluxe   38
Ginger and Tangerine Smoothie   33
Ginger Apple and Cucumber with Lemon   48
Ginger Avocado with Cucumber and Lemon   61
Ginger Lemonade Detox Smoothie   64
Ginger with Lemon Cilantro Detox   66
Ginger with Lemony Detox Drink   61
Goji Berry Wake Up Yoghurt   57
Goji Berry with Banana and Strawberry   65
Grape and Cucumber Green Juice   90
Grape and Green Tea Smoothie   37
Grapy Raspberry Antioxidant Smoothie   53
Grapy Spinach with Berry Yoghurt   80
Grapy Zucchini with Citrus Crush   87
Guava and Orange Jicama Punch   86

H-J

Honey and Cream Berry Shake   34
Honey and Grape Goji Blast   53
Honey and Tofu Berry   32
Honey Soy Blue Smoothie   47
Jicama with almond Milk   85

K

Kale and Celery Green Juice   85
Kale and Fruity Yoghurt Refresher   77
Kale and Mango with Coconut Smoothie   33
Kale Cherry Green Smoothie   45
Kale with Fruity Green Smoothie   44
Kale with Milk Yoghurt   17
Kale with Pineapple and Chia Express   55
Kale with Yoghurt Ginger-Plum   81
Kefir and Beet with Blueberry-Almond   75
Kefir Collagen with Cranberry-Orange   77
Kiwi and Fruity Green Tea Smoothie   73
Kiwi with Mango Smoothie   36
Kiwi with Wheatgrass Detox Smoothie   63

L

Layered Berries and Cream   86
Lemon and Ginger Green Power Juice   90
Lemon and Honey Tangy Blueberry   67
Lemon and Milk Avocado - Swiss Chard   42
Lemon and Milk Sunflower with Spinach   56
Lemon and Mint Breezy Blueberry   55
Lemon and Pear Detox Smoothie   62
Lemony Avocado Yoghurt   18
Lemony Carrot and Veggie Spice   30
Lemony Carrot with Kale   55
Lemony Celery and Parsley Green Juice   89
Lemony Chamomile and Ginger Detox Smoothie   63
Lemony Chia and Ginger Beet   62
Lemony Cucumber Green Machine   74
Lemony Green Tea Detox Smoothie   60
Lemony Kale and Carrot Glass   58
Lemony Veggie Smoothie   71
Lemony Yoghurt and Sherbet Smoothie   36
Lettuce and Mango with Lemon   67
Lime and Milky Detox Smoothie   60
Lime with Mango Greens Smoothie   37
Limeade Cucumber with Cherry   83
Limey Banana with Coconut and Cashew   77
Limey Cucumber with Cilantro and Kale   68
Limey Fruit with Spinach and Cilantro   57
Limey Grape Juice   83
Limey Mango Bliss   49
Limey Pineapple Yoghurt   21
Limey Yoghurt and Cinnamon Smoothie   72

M-N

Mango and Avocado Glowing Skin Glass   54
Mango and Pineapple with Chia Glass   58
Mango with Beets and Protein   81
Maple Berry with Avocado Sunrise Smoothie   67
Milk and Banana Oat Smoothie   24
Milk and Cinnamon with Cocoa Smoothie   78
Milk and Honey with Coconut Almond   34
Milk and Lemon Strawberry   31
Milk with Ginger Berry Flax Smoothie   75
Milky Almond Detox Berry   63
Milky Banana and Butter Delight   47
Milky Beet and Cherry Smoothie   81
Milky Cafe Banana   30
Milky Chia Berry-Basil   86
Milky Chia Oat   20
Milky Chia with Mango Lassi   72
Milky Cinnamon and Coconut Smoothie   26
Milky Dandelion with Blueberry-Oat   80
Milky Flaxseed Berry Burst   74
Milky Flaxseed Spinach   34
Milky Flaxseed Superfood Smoothie   24
Milky Fruit Rainbow Smoothie   44

Milky Kale and Banana Delight   54
Milky Nut and Blueberry 22
Milky Peach and Almond with Blueberry   55
Milky Peach with Chia   50
Milky Peanut Butter and Oatmeal Smoothie 74
Milky Pear and Chia with Protein   69
Milky Soy and Green Smoothie 45
Milky Strawberry Hemp 19
Milky Strawberry Smoothie Sundae   35
Milky Sunflower and Fruit Green   58
Milky Superfood Berry Pudding 25
Minty Apple and Cucumber with Lime 69
Minty Cacao Stick Smoothie   78
Minty Cucumber with Chia and Watermelon 85
Minty Grapefruit Juice 83
Minty Lettuce and Berry with Apple   61
Minty Orange and Mango Green Smoothie   44
Minty Yoghurt with Chocolate Chip 75
Moringa with Hazelnut Detox Smoothie   62
Nectarine and Orange Yoghurt 17
Nut and Berry Wrinkle Fighter   57
Nuts and Gritty Coffee Shake   30

O

Oats with Cashew Butter   20
Orange and Berry Fiesta   46
Orange and Parsley with Mango Detox   65
Orange and Red Banana with Yoghurt 41
Orange Yoghurt Citrus Joy   48
Organic Raspberry and Cucumber Juice 90
Overnight Almond Oats Smoothie 19

P-R

Papaya and Pineapple with Yoghurt 17
Parsley and Apple Anti-Aging Smoothie 53
Peach and Honey with Kale Smoothie 45
Peach and Mint Tea Smoothie 66
Peachy Cinnamon Cobbler 88
Peachy Fruit and Yoghurt 50
Pear with Ginger Pure Gold   56
Pineapple and Milk Flaxseed Supreme   48
Pineapple and Peach Zinc Defense 84
Pineapple Berry Yoghurt Shake 78
Pineapple Hemp Green Smoothie 26
Pineapple Matcha with Mango Smoothie 64
Pineapple with Kale Detox Smoothie   61
Pomegranate and Berry Energizing Electrolytes 76
Pumpkin Chai 84
Radish Blueberry Blast 83
Raspberries and White Chocolate 89
Romaine and Avocado with Jicama   69

S

Spicy Spinach with Pear and Kiwi 85
Spinach and Avocado Detox Smoothie   63
Spinach and Avocado Superfood Smoothie 28
Spinach and Creamy Banana Green Smoothie 42

Spinach and Flaxseed Smoothie   22
Spinach and Grapefruit Smoothie   37
Spinach Berries and Oats Smoothie 42
Spinach Berry with Coconut-Fig 77
Spirulina Mango and Coconut Smoothie   36
Spirulina Mint Superfood Smoothie 25
Squash and Dates Butter Pecan 90
Squash Persimmon Protein Smoothie 79
Stevia and Lemon Garden Smoothie   37
Stevia Strawberry Hemp and Spinach Delight   38
Strawberry and Ceylon Cinnamon Smoothie   36
Strawberry Green Tea with Coconut 54
Strawberry Sherbet Key Lime   43
Strawberry Watermelon and Honey Smoothie 72
Superfood Chocolate Cauliflower   26
Superfood Spinach and Cucumber Smoothie 28
Superfood Vanilla and Pie Smoothie 27
Swiss Chard Pineapple Detox Smoothie   63

T

Tofu and Almond Chocolatey Date   34
Tofu and Banana - Choco Split   47
Tomato and Spinach with Spicy Carrot   69
Tomato with Zucchini Detox Smoothie   62
Tropical Matcha 85
Turmeric and Cauliflower with Mango 84
Turmeric and Cranberry Bliss Detox Smoothie 60
Turmeric with Carrot Detox Smoothie   62
Turmeric with Yoghurt and Lemon Tart 87

V

Vanilla and Chocolate Berry Almond Blast 52
Vanilla Apple Caramel   30
Vanilla Berry Almond Smoothie 28
Vanilla Berry Anti-Aging Smoothie 52
Vanilla Cashew Banana   47
Vanilla Cream Avocado Smoothie 41
Vanilla Milk with Blueberries   17
Vanilla Mixed Berry Yummy   43
Vegan Chocolate Superfood Smoothie 26
Vegetable Fat Burning Smoothie 41

W

Walnut and Banana Oat 21
Walnut and Peach with Cottage Cheese 76
Walnut with Almond Superfood Smoothie 24
Watermelon and Berry Yoghurt 36
Watermelon and Coconut Chia Smoothie 52
Watermelon with Beet and Yoghurt 80
Watermelon with Minty Greens Smoothie 43

Y-Z

Yoghurt and Banana-Zucchini Bread 86
Yoghurt and Chips Raspberry Treat   50
Yoghurt with Citrus Smoothie   72
Yoghurt with Pomegranate-Raspberry 21
Yoghurt with Watermelon Smoothie 53
Zucchini and Papaya with Toasted Coconut 79

CPSIA information can be obtained
at www.ICGtesting.com
Printed in the USA
BVHW011928041121
620792BV00003BA/75